Leisure &
Community
Services

YORK NOTES

Richard II

William Shakespeare

Note by N.H. Keeble

 Lor

D0280020

J 0128 02472 6187

 York Press

BROMLEY PUBLIC LIBRARIES	
02472618	
Cypher	12.07.03
822SHA	£4.50
CENAPB	822·33

Exterior picture of
Raymond Mander
Reconstruction of the Globe Theatre interior reprinted from Hodges:
The Globe Restored (1968) by permission of Oxford University Press

N.H. Keeble is hereby identified as author of this work in accordance with Section 77 of the Copyright, Designs and Patents Act 1988

YORK PRESS
322 Old Brompton Road, London SW5 9JH

PEARSON EDUCATION LIMITED
Edinburgh Gate, Harlow,
Essex CM20 2JE, United Kingdom
Associated companies, branches and representatives throughout the world

© Librairie du Liban *Publishers* and Pearson Education Limited 2000

All rights reserved. No part of this publication may be reproduced, stored in a retrieval system, or transmitted in any form or by any means, electronic, mechanical, photocopying, recording, or otherwise, without either the prior written permission of the Publishers or a licence permitting restricted copying in the United Kingdom issued by the Copyright Licensing Agency Ltd, 90 Tottenham Court Road, London W1P 9HE

First published 2000

ISBN 0–582–42455–0

Designed by Vicki Pacey
Phototypeset by Gem Graphics, Trenance, Mawgan Porth, Cornwall
Colour reproduction and film output by Spectrum Colour
Produced by Addison Wesley Longman China Limited, Hong Kong

CONTENTS

PART ONE

INTRODUCTION

HOW TO STUDY A PLAY

Studying on your own requires self-discipline and a carefully thought-out work plan in order to be effective.

- Drama is a special kind of writing (the technical term is 'genre') because it needs a performance in the theatre to arrive at a full interpretation of its meaning. Try to imagine that you are a member of the audience when reading the play. Think about how it could be presented on the stage, not just about the words on the page.

- Drama is often about conflict of some sort (which may be below the surface). Identify the conflicts in the play and you will be close to identifying the large ideas or themes which bind all the parts together.

- Make careful notes on themes, character, plot and any subplots of the play.

- Why do you like or dislike the characters in the play? How do your feelings towards them develop and change?

- Playwrights find non-realistic ways of allowing an audience to see into the minds and motives of their characters, for example **soliloquy**, aside or music. Consider how such dramatic devices are used in the play.

- Think of the playwright writing the play. Why were these particular arrangements of events, characters and speeches chosen?

- Cite exact sources for all quotations, whether from the text itself or from critical commentaries. Wherever possible find your own examples from the play to back up your own opinions.

- Always express your ideas in your own words.

This York Note offers an introduction to *Richard II* and cannot substitute for close reading of the text and the study of secondary sources.

Richard II is a play about power. During what historians call the early modern period (1500–*c.* 1750) the international Roman Catholic order of Medieval Europe gave way to the secular Europe of nation states which, until the modern experiment of the European Union, ensured that the continent's history would be one of political, military and industrial rivalry. Shakespeare was writing at an early stage in this process, at a time when the rival courts of Europe were enjoying a material splendour, and exercising an authority, far greater than anything known to Medieval monarchs. This was so in Tudor England which, following Henry VIII's break with Rome in the 1530s, developed a new sense of itself as an independent state which looked to its own monarch as the sole authority in determining the political, spiritual and cultural shape of the nation. This expectation came to be embodied most commonly in the 'divine right' theory of monarchy which held that the monarch was divinely chosen and exercised power as God's deputy, unanswerable to any subject. This view was promoted particularly by the Stuart dynasty, which began its English rule shortly after Shakespeare's play was written when, in 1603, James VI of Scotland succeeded Elizabeth I as James I of England.

At the same time as this tendency to exalt absolute monarchy, there was a fascination with how aspiring subjects should conduct themselves under such rulers. Court culture and politics fascinated the Renaissance. A particular impetus was given to this fascination by the thinking of the Italian statesman and political philosopher Niccolò di Bernardo dei Machiavelli, whose writing, in England, was (inaccurately) taken to propose that in pursuit of political influence the ends justified whatever means might be necessary and that achievement of a political objective was the sole criterion by which to assess success. This amorality contributed to the development on the English stage of a recognisable type of character, the Machiavellian villain, ingeniously evolving malevolent plots of fiendish complexity to ensnare his or her victims. Through the outrageousness of these figures, daring to challenge all restraint upon their actions, the cogency and authority of received notions of propriety and morality could be tested.

William Shakespeare created several characters of this type: Iago in *Othello*, for example, or Edmund in *King Lear*; even in his comedies, in a figure such as Don John in *Much Ado About Nothing*. No such character features in *Richard II* (though Northumberland has something of the Machiavellian's disregard for morality and traditional standards), but the play is clearly concerned with interrogating court culture and the exercise of power. The play questions the nature of monarchy, and the extent to which the King is, or is not, bound by any will other than his own, and especially, how far he is answerable to his own subjects for his treatment of them. Fifty years after the writing of *Richard II*, in 1642, this very issue would contribute to the outbreak of the English Civil War. Charles I (James I's son) and the Cavaliers maintained an absolutist notion of monarchy, holding the King answerable to God alone. Their Parliamentarian opponents sought a larger role for Parliament within the constitution, involving the sharing of power between monarch and the people's representative. The issue would not be finally resolved until 1688, when James II (Charles I's second son) fled his throne, and Parliament invited William and Mary to succeed him. Subsequently no monarch could challenge the authority or will of Parliament. All this lay in the future as Elizabethan audiences watched *Richard II* in the late 1590s, but (although those audiences could not know it) the tensions it dramatises ominously portended the seventeenth-century struggles just as, within the fiction of the play, they lead to the fifteenth-century Wars of the Roses.

This is in large part what makes *Richard II* such a resonant and searching play. In Richard is embodied the most exalted notion of kingship. It is a kingship resplendent in its manner of conducting public business, but it is found to be far less impressive in private, and to foster impetuous and tyrannical rule in a monarch immune to criticism. In Henry is embodied quite a different type of authority, based to a degree on popular support, still more on power and opportunity, and on ambition, an ambition perhaps the more sinister for being so reticent about its aspirations – we never know quite what is in Henry's mind, except at the end of the play, and what is disclosed then is far from contentment. Henry may be far more efficient, reliable and sensible than Richard, but he has no acknowledged claim on the crown or pretext to rule. The play's final scene is preoccupied with news of rebels, of war and execution, with Richard's murder, and with Henry's guilt and unease. Setting out to right a wrong (the confiscation of his inheritance as Duke of Lancaster), Henry both perpetrates another wrong by usurping the throne, and apparently establishes an insecure and inauspicious reign. So far is *Richard II* from being a straightforward recommendation of either the divine right of monarchy or the right of the subject to rebel, that the rights and wrongs of the rivalry between the deposed and usurping kings are endlessly intriguing.

The play is, however, rich also in another way. Richard II is Shakespeare's most linguistically accomplished political figure. Henry's taciturnity and reticence serve only the more to highlight Richard's eloquence. His way with words has something to do, as we might expect, with his identification of the duties of kingship with display, pageantry and feudal ceremonial, rather than with duty or responsibility. A king should *sound* like a king; indeed, one suspects that, for Richard, sounding like a king is what constitutes kingship. It has something to do, also, with his tendency towards introspection and self-pity. He would rather reflect upon, and agonise about, his predicament than resolve upon a course of action to remedy it. But if his eloquence has a political and a psychological dimension, it also has a poetic one. He may be politically powerless in the deposition scene (IV.1), but **metaphorical** and **rhetorical** power enables him to play effortlessly with all present, reducing the triumphant Henry to the position of a blustering bystander. There is no escaping the evocative suggestiveness of Richard's words, their figurative allure and melodic **euphony**. Whether this mellifluous allure is truth-telling or truth-concealing is hard to tell with Richard's character. That, too, is part of the play's fascination.

PART TWO

SUMMARIES & COMMENTARIES

Richard II was first published as a **quarto** in 1597. This text (referred to as 'Q1') is unusually free from errors, and may have been printed from William Shakespeare's own manuscript. It therefore forms the basis of modern editions of the play, as it appears to be the copy nearest to Shakespeare's original. Q1 was reprinted twice the following year, 1598 (Q2 and Q3); but each time the type was set, errors entered the text.

None of these **quartos** included the deposition scene (IV.1.154–319). The censor probably thought that, at a time of uncertainty about the succession to the throne (Elizabeth, by then an old woman, was unmarried and childless), it was unwise to allow the public to watch a scene representing the dethroning of an earlier childless monarch, especially since Elizabeth was likened to Richard II by her critics. Those who disapproved of the Queen's reign accused her, as Richard had been accused, of having favourites, of neglecting the kingdom, of being a tyrant and of wasting money – they pointed to Richard's fate as a warning of what might become of her. That *Richard II* was politically dangerous we have clear evidence. When Robert Devereux, Earl of Essex, planned to overthrow Queen Elizabeth, his supporters arranged for *Richard II* to be performed at the Globe Theatre on the eve of the rebellion in February 1601. They undoubtedly felt that the play justified Henry's usurpation and wanted the performance of Shakespeare's play to win popular support in London for their intended dethroning of Elizabeth. In fact, the play refuses to take sides as clearly as this, and in the deposition scene a good deal of sympathy is excited for Richard (see p. 53 of this Note). This may explain why, when the rebellion failed, no action was taken against Shakespeare or his company, the Chamberlain's Men.

Elizabeth died in 1603 and James I succeeded her peacefully five years before Q4 was published in 1608. Hence the security of the monarchy was no longer a delicate matter, and this **quarto** was able to advertise on its title page 'new additions' to the play, namely, the previously unprinted deposition scene. (It is possible that this really was 'new' and that, in the less fraught political atmosphere following Elizabeth's death, Shakespeare revised his play, then adding the deposition scene for the first time. Most commentators, however, believe that, though not printed in Q1, Q2 or Q3, this was part of the original play as performed.) Where the printer of Q4 obtained his copy for this scene is not known, but it was an unreliable source. The deposition scene as it appears in Q4, and in the reprint of 1615 (Q5), is full of errors.

The first **folio** text of 1623 (F1) is based on Q3, and Q5 for some passages at the end of the play. It would not, therefore, be very useful in the ordinary way, since it takes us still further from Q1. However, F1 adds many stage directions not found in the earlier **quartos** and often corrects their texts. It seems probable that these improvements were made by comparing the quartos with the theatre prompt-book (that is, the manuscript copy of the play actually used by the actors) and correcting the printed text where it did not agree with the prompt-book. Furthermore, F1 has a much better text of the deposition scene than Q4 (probably from the same prompt-book). Thus modern editors, basing their texts on Q1, commonly follow F1 for the deposition scene and incorporate into their texts elsewhere those features peculiar to the text of F1 which they believe reflect what Shakespeare actually wrote.

All references to *Richard II* in this Note are to Stanley Wells's New Penguin Shakespeare edition (Penguin Books, 1969; reprinted with a revised further reading section 1997). Act and scene divisions are the same in all modern editions of the play, but line numbers may vary from edition to edition. This variation should not, however, be so great as to prevent anyone using a different edition from finding a reference in the text.

All references to Shakespeare's other plays are to *The Norton Shakespeare*, general editor Stephen Greenblatt (Norton, 1997), but again, it should be easy to locate these references in any good edition of Shakespeare.

ACT I: RICHARD AS KING (APRIL 1398 – FEBRUARY 1399)

In the spring of 1398 Richard II, King of England, has come to hear an accusation of treason laid by his cousin, Henry Bolingbroke, Duke of Hereford, against Thomas Mowbray, Duke of Norfolk. Henry charges Mowbray with misusing money given him by the King to pay his soldiers, with instigating all the plots against Richard during the last eighteen years, and, in particular, with being responsible for the murder of Richard's and Henry's uncle, Thomas of Woodstock, Duke of Gloucester. Mowbray denies the charges and Richard, unable to reconcile the two men, appoints St Lambert's Day (17 September) for them to settle the issue by single combat. Before that occurs (in I.3), we learn in I.2 from John of Gaunt (Duke of Lancaster, Henry's father and a brother of Gloucester) that Richard himself was implicated in Gloucester's death. Gaunt refuses the pleas of the Duchess of Gloucester to avenge Gloucester himself, saying that no subject may punish God's deputy on earth, the King. As the trial by combat is about to begin in I.3, it is unexpectedly halted by Richard, who banishes both combatants – Mowbray for life, Henry for ten years, which he reduces to six when he sees Gaunt's sorrow. In private conversation with his close friends in I.4, Richard shows himself jealous of Henry's popular support; resolved to finance his expedition against Irish rebels by illegal and tyrannical means; and callous when he hears that Gaunt is dying.

ACT II: THE BEGINNING OF RICHARD'S DECLINE (FEBRUARY 1399 – JULY 1399)

The act begins with Gaunt foretelling that Richard's extravagant and irresponsible way of life cannot last long. Gaunt is deeply distressed at the way the England he loves is neglected and mistreated by the King. When Richard enters, Gaunt rebukes him, but this only provokes Richard's anger. Shortly after Gaunt leaves the stage his death is reported and Richard immediately plans to seize his uncle's wealth (rightfully now the inheritance of Gaunt's son, Henry) to finance an Irish campaign. Gaunt's brother, Edmund of Langley, Duke of York, protests at this, and foretells dire consequences if Richard denies Henry his rights, but Richard is not dissuaded. As the scene ends, we hear that Henry already has an invasion force prepared to sail for England as soon as Richard leaves for Ireland. In the next scene, II.2, the air of foreboding steadily grows as the Queen, Isabel, is filled with fearful apprehensions, the news is brought that Henry has landed, and York admits that, as Governor of England in Richard's absence, he is ill-prepared to resist him. The scene ends with Richard's favourites, Bushy, Bagot and Green, resolving to flee for fear of popular vengeance against them. In II.3, Henry and his aide Northumberland proceed through England, gathering support, until they come to Berkeley Castle, where York tries to persuade Henry to lay down his arms. Henry protests that he has come not to harm Richard but to gain his rights as Duke of Lancaster; and York admits he can do nothing to stop him. In II.4 the Welsh army, which had been gathered to fight for Richard, tires of waiting for the King to return from Ireland and disbands. Richard is now effectively powerless to confront Henry.

ACT III: THE SURRENDER OF RICHARD
        (JULY 1399 – AUGUST 1399)

Henry, at Bristol Castle, executes Bushy and Green, who had taken refuge there (III.1). In III.2 Richard finally returns from Ireland and has high hopes that his mere presence will win support, but a succession of discouraging reports (the disbanding of the Welsh army, the extent of popular and noble support for Henry, the execution of his favourites and the desertion of York to Henry) plunge him into despair and he discharges his followers. At Flint Castle, in III.3, he immediately grants Henry's demand for his rights as Duke of Lancaster, although he is convinced that Henry is really after the crown. He leaves for London, in Henry's power. The act ends with the 'garden scene' (III.4) in which the Queen hears of Henry's success from a gardener and decides to go to London herself.

ACT IV: THE DEPOSITION OF RICHARD
        (SEPTEMBER 1399 – DECEMBER 1399)

At the beginning of the act, nobles argue fiercely about who was, or was not, responsible for Gloucester's death and Henry resolves that the various charges should be settled by combat. York, bringing the news that Richard has agreed to give up his crown, hails Henry as King Henry IV.

At this the Bishop of Carlisle protests that no subject can judge a king, let alone force him to abdicate. For this he is charged with treason. Richard enters, and does give Henry the crown, but he cannot bring himself to make a public declaration of his faults. He is deeply disturbed in his mind and, although Henry has arranged the whole affair and has his way, it is Richard who is at the centre of the scene and who wins our sympathy as he shames the nobles present as his betrayers. The act ends with the Abbot of Westminster, the Bishop of Carlisle and the Duke of Aumerle (York's son) discussing a plot to overthrow Henry and restore Richard.

ACT V: REBELLION AND THE DEATH OF RICHARD
        (DECEMBER 1399 – MARCH 1400)

In V.1 the Queen meets Richard on his way to the Tower. Their conversation is interrupted by Northumberland, who orders Richard to Pomfret Castle in Yorkshire, and the Queen to France. They take a final farewell. In V.2 York discovers from Aumerle the plot against Henry and, as he has sworn loyalty to Henry and guaranteed Aumerle's loyalty to the new king, he is determined, despite the pleas of the Duchess of York, to go immediately to reveal the treason to Henry. The Duchess sends Aumerle to reach Henry before York, and intends to follow as quickly as she can. At the beginning of V.3 we find Henry troubled by the reckless behaviour of his son who, it seems, will not make a very suitable heir to the throne. Aumerle then bursts in and, in private, asks for, and receives, Henry's pardon before Henry knows what it is he was going to do. But when York arrives, the plot is revealed, and York insists Aumerle should not be forgiven. He is interrupted by the Duchess knocking on the door, and she, just as vehemently, begs that Aumerle should be pardoned. Henry, not quite sure whether to take all this clamour and contradiction seriously, does pardon Aumerle, but arranges for the other rebels to be pursued. In V.4 Sir Piers of Exton determines to assassinate Richard in order to relieve Henry of the risk posed by the continuing survival of the former king. Alone in his prison, in V.5, Richard meditates on his sorrow. When the murderers come, he puts up a brave fight, but it is in vain. In the last scene of the play we hear that the rebellion has been crushed. When Sir Piers brings Richard's body to Henry, he receives no thanks. On the contrary, Henry is filled with shame and guilt, and the play ends with him planning a crusade 'To wash this blood off from my guilty hand'.

ACT I

SCENE 1   **Henry Bolingbroke charges Thomas Mowbray with treason and Richard appoints a day for the case to be settled by combat**

The play opens with Richard fulfilling the monarch's most important function, dispensing justice. He has come to hear a charge of treason made by his cousin, Henry Bolingbroke, Duke of Hereford, against Thomas Mowbray, Duke of Norfolk. Bolingbroke speaks vigorously, but it is some time before he makes specific charges. When he does they are three in number: that Mowbray has misused for his own advantage money given him by the King; that he has been responsible for all the plots against the King during the past eighteen years; and that he is guilty of murdering Richard's and Henry's uncle, Thomas of Woodstock, Duke of Gloucester. Mowbray denies these charges, and in return himself accuses Bolingbroke of treason. Richard tries to reconcile the two men, but his efforts are in vain. He therefore appoints a date (St Lambert's Day) for them to settle the matter by trial by combat.

> Richard is himself to be at the centre of this play and the drama begins by presenting him in his full royal majesty. Theatrically, the presentation of a full court in the first scene makes a spectacular opening to the play. Throughout this scene Richard conducts himself as befits a king: he speaks royally, claims to be impartial and seems anxious to restore peace and goodwill. Yet there are already signs that he is not quite the just king he seems. As Shakespeare's audience probably knew (and would, in any case, learn in the next scene), Richard had himself ordered Mowbray to kill Gloucester. If Henry knows of Mowbray's guilt, then he may well know of Richard's. That he does know is perhaps suggested by his reference to the biblical murder of Abel (line 104): Abel was slain by his close kinsman Cain, as Gloucester was by his kinsman Richard. That Richard fears his own guilt may be disclosed is suggested in

line 109, where he sees Henry's accusation as an attack on himself.
The fact that Richard denies (even **ironically**) that Henry is his heir
(line 116) indicates that the idea that Henry is after the crown has
crossed his mind. Thus behind the formal surface of the occasion
there is a bitter family quarrel: it is Henry – Edward III's grandson,
like Richard – who is really the champion of justice, and not
Richard, the King. The frequent references to murder and blood
further create an atmosphere of suspense and foreboding.

Historically we know that Bolingbroke's 'appeal', or accusation, was
made on 29 April 1398, at Windsor, though neither the time nor
the place is mentioned in the play.

s.d. **King Richard** Richard of Bordeaux was born in 1367, the only son of
Edward, the Black Prince, who was the eldest son and heir of Edward III

John of Gaunt John of Gaunt (Ghent; he was born in Flanders in 1340),
Duke of Lancaster, was the fourth son of Edward III, thus Richard's uncle

Lord Marshal the Duke of Surrey (who appears in IV.1) acted on behalf of
Mowbray, on this occasion as the Lord Marshal (in charge of heraldry and
state occasions); but whether Shakespeare meant to identify the two
characters is not clear (see pages 26 and 54 of this Note)

2 **band** bond

3 **Henry Hereford** Henry of Bolingbroke (his birthplace in Lincolnshire), Duke
of Hereford (in Elizabethan pronunciation, only two syllables, as 'Herford')
was born in 1367 to John of Gaunt's first wife, Blanche of Lancaster; he is
thus Richard's exact contemporary and his cousin

4 **late appeal** recent accusation of treason. Henry accused Mowbray of treason
at a parliament at Shrewsbury in January 1398 and both men were ordered
to appear before the King to settle the matter

5 **our leisure would not let us hear** our want of leisure would not let us hear. It
was a convention for monarchs to use the plural forms of pronouns

6 **Thomas Mowbray** Thomas Mowbray, Duke of Norfolk, was born around 1366

9 **If he appeal the Duke on ancient malice** whether he accuses Mowbray
because of some old grudge

13–14 **On ... malice** it is because he has detected some clear threat posed to your
highness by Mowbray, and not because of any confirmed hatred he bears
him

18 **High-stomached** proud, stubborn

s.d. **Bolingbroke** pronounced (and spelled) 'Bullingbrook' in Shakespeare's time

22 **Each day still better other's happiness** may each day so improve on the happiness of previous days

24 **Add an immortal title to your crown** until you receive immortal happiness in heaven

26 **the cause you come** the cause about which you come

28 **thou** the informal language of affection, used between members of a family, changed to the formal 'you' when Richard is trying to assert his authority (line 186). Modern English has lost this distinction which was possible in the singular ('you' in line 25 is plural)

30 **heaven be the record** may heaven be the witness; Henry begins by clearing himself of the suspicion of personal malice which Richard had expressed in lines 8–10

32 **Tendering** valuing, cherishing

33 **from other** from all other motives

37 **My body shall make good upon this earth** I will prove by mortal combat

38 **divine** immortal

39 **miscreant** literally 'unbeliever', but used as a general term of contempt

40 **good** high in rank (the idea is developed in lines 41–2)

46 **right-drawn** drawn from the sheath in a just cause

48 **woman's war** fighting with words, verbal argument

51 **hot** both heated in anger and warm since Henry is alive; the blood must be 'cooled' in death by Mowbray's sword

55 **reins and spurs** to hold the reins loosely and apply spurs to a horse would make it gallop; Mowbray means that Richard's royal presence prevents him from replying in passionate anger

56 **post** ride swiftly (post horses were kept at inns on main roads to allow messengers to travel quickly by changing horses at frequent intervals)

58 **high blood's royalty** his kinship to Richard

59 **let him be** assuming that he is (it would be dangerous to directly accuse a member of the King's family of treason)

62 **maintain** prove

65 **inhabitable** not habitable, i.e. uninhabitable

s.d. **gage** pledge; by throwing down an object (usually a glove) the challenger pledged to fight whoever took it up

70 **Disclaiming here the kindred of the King** taking up Mowbray's words of lines 58–9, Henry rejects the protection of his royal blood

74 **honour's pawn** the pledge of honour referred to at line 69
79 **Which gently laid my knighthood on my shoulder** men were created knights by being touched on each shoulder ('dubbed') with a sword. Mowbray was probably knighted by Richard, which would make the reference a polite compliment which seems to have secured Richard's goodwill in lines 84–6. 'Gently' here means 'nobly'
80–1 **any ... trial** any proper manner or chivalric form of knightly combat
85 **inherit us** possess us with, make us think
87 **Look what** whatever
88 **nobles** gold coins (each worth a third of a pound)
89 **lendings** pay
90 **lewd employments** improper use
97 **Fetch** derive
100 **the Duke of Gloucester's death** Thomas of Woodstock (his birthplace), Duke of Gloucester, was born in 1355, the seventh and youngest son of Edward III; he was thus the brother of Gaunt and York and the uncle of Richard and Henry. An opponent of Richard's policies, he was charged with treason and killed at Calais in 1397, almost certainly by Mowbray on Richard's orders; this was the view of Shakespeare's time, found in Holinshed (see Shakespeare's Use of Sources), and put forward by Gaunt in the next scene (I.2.37–41). This third charge by Henry is the crucial one, and (as Richard's reply, line 109, shows) the one that comes near the King
101 **Suggest his soon-believing adversaries** persuaded Gloucester's enemies, who were only too ready to believe it, that he was guilty of treason
103 **Sluiced out** let out
104 **Abel** in the biblical story the innocent Abel was slain by his brother Cain, who was jealous of Abel's favour with God, and Abel's blood cried out from the ground for vengeance (Genesis 4:1–16). The reference can be seen as a sly attack on Richard – as Abel was slain by his kinsman Cain, so Gloucester was slain by his kinsman Richard; it stresses Gloucester's innocence (by likening him to Abel) and Mowbray's wickedness (as the first murderer, Cain is a particularly horrible figure), and it underlines the fact that, despite the formality of the occasion, this is a *family* quarrel
107 **the glorious worth of my descent** the nobility of my family line
109 **pitch** the highest point of a falcon's flight. This is a crucial line, for in seeing that Henry aims high, Richard recognises here that Henry's previous speech had been directed at him, the highest in the

land; it may be that Richard already suspects Henry of ambitious designs on the crown – whether or not Henry *does* yet have them we do not know

113 **this slander of his blood** this disgrace (Henry) to his (Richard's) blood

120 **partialize** make partial, make me favour him

126 **receipt** money received

130 **remainder of a dear account** payment outstanding on a large debt

131 **fetch his queen** Mowbray went to France in 1395 to arrange Richard's marriage to Isabel; he means that Richard had not paid him back his expenses for this trip

133–4 **I ... case** Mowbray probably intends Henry and the court to understand that he failed in his duty because he did not manage to save Gloucester (which is, in fact, a gross misrepresentation)

137 **ambush** no details are known of this, but that Mowbray should admit such a misdemeanour would make him seem honest to the watching nobles

144 **recreant** cowardly

145 **Which in myself I boldly will defend** which charge (i.e. that the accusation is groundless spite) I personally will prove

146 **interchangeably** in return (Mowbray is now accusing, or 'appealing', Henry of treason in his turn)

149 **Even in the best blood** by shedding the blood

150 **In haste whereof** that this may happen quickly

156 **conclude** come to an understanding

157 **no month** through astrology, doctors were thought to know when was the best time of year to treat their patients by bleeding them; throughout this speech Richard plays on the idea of the letting of blood (i.e. medicinal bleeding) and blood-letting (i.e. fighting)

161–2 **Throw down ... throw down** Henry and Mowbray have evidently picked up each other's gages

164 **boot** remedy

167 **The one my duty owes** as a loyal subject I owe you my life

167–9 **my fair name ... have** Mowbray means that Richard shall not command him to submit and so deny him a good name after he is dead

170 **baffled** insulted, disgraced

174 **Lions make leopards tame** a lion figured in the King's coat of arms, and a leopard in Mowbray's

175 **not change his spots** the proverb 'The leopard cannot change his spots' derives from the Bible (Jeremiah 13:23)

179 **gilded loam** painted earth

182 **in one** together

189 **impeach my height** disgrace my breeding

190 **outdared** cowed, i.e. overcome by Henry's boldness in accusing him

191 **feeble wrong** cowardly act (as submitting to Mowbray)

192 **sound so base a parle** Henry employs an **image** from the blowing (sounding) of trumpets to stop a battle

193 **motive** organ, i.e. his tongue

194 **in his** to its (i.e. the tongue's): the possessive pronoun 'its' did not come into common use until the seventeenth century

199 **Saint Lambert's Day** 17 September

202 **atone** reconcile

203 **Justice design the victor's chivalry** let God's justice so guide the courage of the just man that he will be victorious; the theory behind trial by combat

205 **home** England, as distinct from the troubles abroad in Ireland, of which we hear in I.4.38

SCENE 2   Gaunt refuses to avenge Gloucester's murder

John of Gaunt refuses the pleas of the Duchess of Gloucester to avenge the murder of her husband. She argues that not only is this owed by Gaunt to his father and brother, but that his own self-interest should prompt it. Gaunt reveals that Richard himself was implicated in Gloucester's death and asserts that no subject may judge God's deputy on earth, the King.

The matter of this scene is not in the sources of the play (see Shakespeare's Use of Sources): clearly, then, Shakespeare had a particular reason for inventing it and inserting it here. As an intimate and heartfelt dialogue, it does serve to contrast in manner and tone with the pageantry of both I.1 and I.3. Furthermore, by disclosing Richard's involvement in Gloucester's death, the scene reveals that, far from being the impartial and just figure he would appear to be, the King is himself deeply concerned in the quarrel. This will have a bearing on his actions in I.3. This scene also continues the **imagery** of blood and the references to Edward III which were introduced in I.1.

s.d. **Duchess of Gloucester** Eleanor Bohun, *c.* 1360–99

1 **the part I had in Woodstock's blood** John of Gaunt and Thomas of Woodstock were brothers

2 **solicit** tempt

4–5 **But ... correct** it is the responsibility of Richard, as King, to punish ('correction') the murderer but as he is himself implicated ('Which made the fault') there is nothing we can do ('cannot correct')

7 **they** God and the angels

9 **Finds brotherhood in thee no sharper spur?** are you no more anxious than that to act like a brother?

11 **Edward** Edward III (1327–77), father of Gaunt, York and Gloucester, and grandfather of Richard and Henry

13 **seven fair branches springing from one root** to the image of the vials of blood (line 12) is added that of a genealogical table or 'tree': Elizabethan tables placed the founder of the family at the foot or 'root' (not at the top, as in a modern table) and showed the descendants as 'branches' of the tree

14 **are dried by nature's course** have died a natural death of old age

15 **by the destinies cut** died violently, as in battle

21 **envy** hatred

23 **mettle** substance

self same

27–8 **thou ... life** this expresses the same thought as in lines 24–5: since Edward's blood was in Gloucester's veins, Gaunt's acceptance of Gloucester's murder is acceptance of the death of his own father

29 **patience** the Christian virtue of accepting humbly whatever God ordains

despair the sin of supposing one's condition is beyond God's mercy

30 **suffering** allowing

30–1 **In ... life** the Duchess appeals to Gaunt's self-interest: to allow the murderer to escape is to risk his own life (see lines 35–6)

31 **naked** open, obvious

33 **mean** ordinary, common

37 **God's substitute** the King, thought to be divinely appointed (see Richard's view in III.2.54–62 and III.3.72–81, and the Bishop of Carlisle's in IV.1.121–9)

40–1 **I ... minister** it was generally accepted in the Elizabethan period that no subject could judge or rebel against a true king

42 **Where then, alas, may I complain myself?** to whom, then, may I complain?

46 **cousin** relative, kinsman
fell cruel, ruthless
49 **if misfortune miss the first career** if Mowbray is not killed with the first charge
51 **courser** horse
52 **lists** the ground between the spectators where the combatants would fight
53 **caitiff recreant** disloyal coward
54 **Thy sometimes** she who was formerly your
58 **boundeth** rebounds
59 **Not with the empty hollowness, but weight** a ball bounces because it is hollow, but her grief rebounds because it is so heavy with sadness
66 **Pleshey** Thomas, Duke of Gloucester, had a house in this Essex village
69 **offices** servants' quarters
71 **Therefore commend me** since the Duke of York would find only sorrow at Pleshey, rather than invite him to come the Duchess asks Gaunt to commend her to him
74 **The last leave** because she expects to die of grief (as occurs, II.2.97)

SCENE 3   Richard halts the trial by combat between Bolingbroke and Mowbray and banishes both men

After the pause of I.2, we return to the pageantry of I.1, now in no doubt about Richard's involvement in this affair. It is 17 September 1398 and the lists have been prepared at Coventry for the trial by combat arranged to determine whether Mowbray is the traitor Henry claims. Shakespeare, following Holinshed closely (see Shakespeare's Use of Sources), gives full weight to the formal splendour of the occasion: the scene builds up tension slowly through the chivalric formalities of the identification of the combatants, the statement of the cause of the quarrel and the swearing of oaths, the ceremonial leave-takings, the arming of the combatants and the final declaration by the heralds until, at last, the Lord Marshal orders the trumpets to sound to begin the contest. At this moment, Richard suddenly intervenes, prevents the fight and banishes both men from England – Mowbray for life, Bolingbroke for ten years (which the King reduces to six when he sees Gaunt's sorrow).

This sudden turn of events is dramatic precisely because it so unexpectedly disrupts the formality of the scene – but why does

Richard intervene and banish both Henry Bolingbroke and Thomas Mowbray, when (as he himself had said, I.1.25–7) one of them must be innocent? Some critics have found here evidence of Richard's wilfulness, his unstable nature and tendency to rule in an irrational and arbitrary fashion. That Richard, on the spur of the moment, later reduces the length of Henry's banishment (lines 208–12) seems to support the view that he acts from mere whim, enjoying his power in an irresponsible way. Henry's comment (lines 213–15) underlines this arbitrary power, and Gaunt's reply (lines 216–32) looks very much like a pointed rebuke showing Richard that he is not, in fact, *all*-powerful – he cannot keep Gaunt young.

It is, however, possible to take another view of this event, namely, that Richard is in fact very much in control, and makes a masterstroke of policy by intervening before either man is proved innocent. This quarrel concerns him closely: both Mowbray (as his agent in the murder) and Bolingbroke (who seeks to redress this wrong) pose a threat to him. Richard himself detects ambition in them (lines 129–30) and is anxious that they should not conspire together against him (lines 178–90). By banishing *both*, he not only removes both threats but also retains the appearance of impartiality. Had they fought, the victor, whichever it might be, would have been in a very strong position to challenge Richard – Mowbray by threatening to reveal the truth, Henry by questioning Richard's own part in Gloucester's death. Of course, the plan (if such it be) does not work: but that Richard is capable of such deviousness will become evident in the very next scene. Why, though, Henry should be banished for a shorter period than Mowbray is not clear, whichever view is taken of Richard's action. Perhaps we are to suppose that Henry's popularity means that if Richard were to act too severely against him there would be a risk of popular rebellion in support of Henry; but the evidence for this popularity only comes later (I.4.23–36).

The scene ends with remarkable dignity and nobility in the responses of both men to the King's treatment of them, and in Gaunt's expression of grief. It is very difficult not to feel that all three behave with greater genuine nobility than Richard.

s.d. **Duke of Aumerle** Edward of Norwich (*c.* 1373–1415), York's eldest son (and so Henry's cousin, line 64), is to play a significant part in the fifth act. Here, he serves the Lord Marshal as High Constable. Aumerle's noble and brave death at the battle of Agincourt, by which point he has become Duke of York, is remembered in *Henry V*, IV.6.3–34

2 **enter in** the stage itself is imagined as the lists, the field of combat, to which the appellants enter from either side; the members of the play's audience thus find themselves in the position of spectators at the trial

4 **Stays but** waits only for

s.d. **Bushy, Bagot, and Green** Sir John Bushy (or Bussy), Sir William Bagot and Sir Henry Green were councillors who actively promoted Richard's policies in Parliament; in the play they are less important as individuals than as representatives of the favourites who advised Richard badly and reaped personal gain from his corrupt rule. Bushy and Green were executed at Bristol in 1399 by the supporters of Henry (III.1.1–35); Bagot escaped to Ireland and died in 1407, but there is some confusion over Bagot in *Richard II* (see pages 41, 46 and 54 of this Note)

9–10 **orderly ... cause** proceed in due order to have him swear his cause is just

11 **say who thou art** the formal identification of combatants was necessary since a knight in full armour with his visor down would not be recognisable

18 **defend** forbid

19 **truth** the word conveys more than mere honesty, for to be 'true' was the distinguishing mark of the chivalric knight: integrity, loyalty, trustworthiness and nobility are all implied

20 **my succeeding issue** Mowbray defends his descendants from the shame of an ancestor who was a traitor

25 **truly** on behalf of the truth

28 **plated in habiliments of war** enclosed in plate armour

30 **Depose him in** swear him to

57 **blood** kinsman

58 **Lament we may, but not revenge thee dead** should Henry die, his death would not be avenged, as his guilt will have been proved

59 **profane** waste by shedding needlessly

66 **cheerly** happily, but stronger in sense than its modern equivalent 'cheerfully': there is a suggestion of boldness and bravery

67 **regreet** welcome; at line 142 the word is used differently

68 **daintiest last** English feasts ended with sweet confections

70 **regenerate** reborn

71 **two-fold** Henry enjoys both his own youth and that of his father reborn in him (line 70)

73 **proof** 'proof armour' was armour whose strength had been proved in combat; Henry is asking his father to give this guarantee of strength to his own armour by Gaunt's prayers

75 **That it may enter Mowbray's waxen coat** so that it may pierce Mowbray's coat of mail as if it were soft as wax

76 **furbish** literally, to clean and polish armour: Henry means that his success would give new brilliance to the name of John of Gaunt

81 **amazing** stunning (the word had a much stronger sense in Shakespeare's time than it does today)

85–7 **However ... gentleman** an understandable boast, but not one which the theory of trial by combat would support: the defeated party was deemed to be 'proven' guilty simply by virtue of being defeated

91 **More** Mowbray means that no freed captive was ever more joyous than he at the prospect of this combat

92 **feast** festival

95 **jest** sport

98 **couchèd** lying, lodged

101 **Receive thy lance** combatants did not bring their own lances but received them from the Marshal, who would ensure their equal length

102 **Strong as a tower in hope** a biblical phrase deriving from Psalms 61:3

106 **On pain to be found false** on pain of being himself found false (if he fails to defeat Mowbray)

112 **approve** prove

116 **Attending** waiting for

117 **set forward** it is just possible that horses were actually used in the Elizabethan theatre

s.d. **warder** ceremonial staff or baton

120 **chairs** after formally identifying himself, a knight at a trial would sit in a ceremonial chair within a small tent or pavilion until the contest began

122 **While we return** until we inform

s.d. **flourish** trumpet call

125 **For that** so that

131 **set on you** set you on

134 **Which** the syntax of this passage is confused: 'Which' seems to refer to 'peace' (line 132), but if so, then peace, having been 'roused up' (line 134) goes on to 'fright fair peace' (line 137), which makes little sense. Some critics feel that the confusion indicates that Richard is hiding his true motives (see scene summary), but there is probably textual corruption here. The general thrust (that this combat might lead to further conflict and so permanently endanger peace) is clear

139 **you our** you from our

140 **upon pain of life** upon pain of forfeiting your life (i.e. if Hereford returns before the term is up)

142 **regreet** greet again

143 **stranger** foreign (not used as a comparative adjective here)

147 **point on** aim at

150 **determinate** put an end to

151 **dear** dreadful, dire

156 **A dearer merit, not so deep a maim** a better reward and not so deep an injury

159 **forty years** Mowbray was in fact only thirty-three years old in 1398

162 **viol** a stringed musical instrument played with a bow

163 **Or like a cunning instrument cased up** or like an instrument capable of producing subtle sounds shut up in its box, silent and useless

165 **That knows no touch** who does not know how to play it

168-9 **And ... me** Mowbray's ignorance of foreign languages will prevent him from talking (and so is the gaoler of his tongue)

170 **I am too old to fawn upon a nurse** I am too old to learn a new language as would a child from its wet-nurse

172 **speechless death** the dead are silent, and as Mowbray will speak his native language no more, his exile will be a death

174 **It boots thee not to be compassionate** either 'It is no use being sorry for yourself' or 'It is no use asking for pity'

179 **on our royal sword** where a sword's blade and hilt join the hand-guard a cross is formed, so an oath sworn on a sword is sworn on the supreme symbol of Christianity

181 **Our part** the duty you owe me as God's deputy

193 **so far as to mine enemy** so much I can say to my enemy

196 **frail sepulchre of our flesh** weak tomb (of the soul) made of flesh

202 **book of life** it was thought that the names of those to enjoy the bliss of heaven were written in God's book (see Revelation 3:5)

206–7 **Now ... way** I cannot go astray now for, with the exception of returning to England, I am free to wander anywhere in the world

208 **glasses** mirrors (they reflect Gaunt's feelings)

214 **wanton** rich, luxuriant

220 **Can change their moons, and bring their times about** can pass through the cycles of the moon's waxing and waning necessary to complete the term of banishment

221 **oil-dried lamp** a lamp without oil (i.e. which would not light)
time-bewasted wasted by time

223 **inch of taper** a taper is a thin candle: Gaunt likens the short period of life he has left to the last inch of a candle before it burns out

224 **blindfold death** the figure of Death was frequently pictured as blind; the traditional **symbol** of death, a skull, is eyeless; and the dead cannot see. In this instance, for Gaunt, death would be the blindfold preventing him from seeing his son

230 **pilgrimage** journey, passage (of time)

231 **current** valid, acceptable

234 **Whereto thy tongue a party-verdict gave** your voice contributed to the discussion which led to our decision

240 **smooth** mitigate, excuse, gloss over

241 **partial slander** the accusation of being biased in Henry's favour

243 **looked when** expected that, waited for

244 **to make mine own** in making my own son

249 **Cousin, farewell!** since Aumerle accompanies Henry (I.4.3–4), it is odd that he should take his leave of him here
What presence must not know what we shall not be able to learn from you personally (since Henry will be in exile)

250 **let paper show** write in a letter

251–2 **My lord ... your side** it is curious that the Duke of Surrey, who acted as Lord Marshal on this occasion (see note on the stage direction at the beginning of I.1), should be so friendly to Henry here, when he appears later (IV.1.60–71) as a supporter of Richard: it may be that Shakespeare either did not know, or had forgotten, that the Lord Marshal *was* the Duke of Surrey, and so thought of the two figures as two distinct characters, which is how they are listed in the *dramatis personae* in most modern editions

257 **To breathe** in expressing

258 **grief** both 'sorrow' and 'cause for sorrow'

266–7 **Esteem ... return** as a jewel shines brighter against its metal setting (its 'foil') Henry should think of his exile as the foil against which to set off the happiness of his homecoming

269 **remember me what a deal of world** remind me what a distance

271–4 **Must ... grief?** Henry will, like an apprentice, learn the ways of foreign travel; having mastered them like a journeyman (a qualified craftsman), when his exile is over (to 'have freedom' was the technical term for the end of an apprenticeship) he will not, like a true journeyman, be proud of the achievement but will see it merely as an undesirably full acquaintance with sorrow

272 **passages** experiences

275–8 **All ... necessity** proverbial wisdom claiming that, since all the earth is God's, one can never be truly banished as it is impossible to leave God's sight and so the proper course is to benefit from whatever circumstances we find ourselves in

282 **purchase** gain

286 **Look what** whatever

289 **presence** the presence chamber, where the monarch received visitors
strewed covered (the floors of rooms were covered with rushes)

291 **measure** dance

292 **gnarling** snarling

296 **cloy** stifle by over-indulging

299 **fantastic** imaginary

300 **apprehension** conception, knowledge

300–1 **O ... worse** awareness of the good only makes us feel its lack the more keenly

302–3 **Fell ... sore** in line 292 sorrow had been conceived of as a snarling animal which bites, and that **metaphor** is continued here: cruel ('Fell') sorrow's teeth make the most festering wounds ('doth never rankle more') when he bites but does not make a deep wound like that a surgeon cuts ('lanceth') to cure a poisoned abscess ('sore'). Henry seems to feel that the bitterness of sorrow can (like a surgeon's knife, which cuts sharply to heal) be its own cure if it is recognised for what it is, and that Gaunt, by offering weak consolation, threatens not to end Henry's sorrow but only to dull it (or blunt the surgeon's knife) so that it will linger on and on

SCENE 4   **Richard reveals his determination to use whatever means are available to further his political ends, and, in particular, to seize Gaunt's estate**

In private conversation with Bagot, Green and Aumerle, Richard expresses intense resentment of Henry's popularity with the common people. He recognises that Henry has already usurped his place in the people's hearts. We then learn that, to finance his expedition against the Irish rebels, Richard plans to use unjust and tyrannical methods, giving his favourites power to raise taxes for themselves in return for ready money and raising forced loans from his wealthy subjects. When, at the end of the scene, Richard learns from Bushy that Gaunt is dying, he callously hopes that he will die quickly so that his wealth can be seized.

This short scene achieves an effect of striking contrast. As Shakespeare had varied the dramatic pace and tone by following the court scene of I.1 with the private anguish of I.2, so now the pageantry of I.3 is followed by a very different kind of scene: after his commanding performance at the formal state occasion we have just witnessed, Richard is shown talking in confidence to his closest friends. A very different side to Richard is revealed when he is not acting the King before an audience. All his nobility of manner and fine eloquence has gone as he speaks with selfish disregard for everyone else. He has only scorn for his subjects, derision for Henry, and heartlessness for Gaunt. It is now clear that the concern for his uncle which he expressed in I.3.208–11 was sheer hypocrisy. Building on earlier suspicions, this scene thus confirms that Richard is not all that he seems publicly.

The extent of Henry's popularity explains why there had been hints earlier that Richard feared Henry (I.1.109, I.3.129–33), and perhaps why Richard banished him. There may even be a suggestion that Richard does not intend that Henry shall ever return (lines 20–2).

1 **We did observe** Richard enters in mid-conversation; what was observed is mentioned in line 24

6 **for me** by me, for my part

9 **hollow** Aumerle is much colder towards Henry than in I.3.249–50: the **irony** of line 3 indicates that he does not consider Henry noble, and now he claims that their parting was 'hollow' (i.e. without true sorrow) and that any tears were the result not of feeling but of the cold wind

14–15 **To counterfeit ... grave** to pretend to be so afflicted by grief that words were as impossible to utter as if they had been buried in a grave made by sorrow

22 **Whether our kinsman come to see his friends** Richard means by 'friends' noble relatives: it is doubtful whether Henry will see them when he returns because, as Richard sarcastically goes on to explain, Henry seems to prefer the common people; there is also the more sinister implication that Richard does not intend that he will ever be allowed to return – the possibility that Richard plans to have him murdered cannot be excluded

27 **slaves** a term of contempt for the common people

29 **underbearing** endurance

30 **As 'twere to banish their affects with him** as if he were trying to take into exile ('banish') the affections ('affects') of the people with him

33 **And had the tribute of his supple knee** Henry bends his knee to them

35 **our** Richard's (i.e. not Richard's and Aumerle's)

reversion a legal term for the return of property to its rightful owner on the death of a tenant

36 **next degree in** next object of (upon Richard's death)

37 **go these thoughts** let these thoughts go too

39 **Expedient manage** quick and efficient arrangements

43 **too great a court** maintaining the court on too lavish a scale

45 **farm** in return for an immediate sum of money, Richard will confer on certain people the revenues and taxes due to him as King

48 **substitutes** deputies, officers

blank charters legal documents which wealthy subjects were made to sign, whereby they promised to pay the King unspecified sums of money; the King (or his agents) wrote in a figure *after* the document was signed

52 **presently** immediately

55 **taken** fallen ill

58 **Ely House** the palace of the Bishop of Ely at Holborn, in London

61 **lining** while Richard refers to the contents, which 'line' Gaunt's treasure chests ('coffers'), the word fits with the 'coats' that follow

ACT II

SCENE 1   **Upon Gaunt's death, Richard seizes his uncle's estate (which is rightfully Henry Bolingbroke's inheritance) and, as he leaves for his Irish campaign amid ominous signs of growing discontent with his rule, there is news that Henry is poised to invade England**

The scene opens with York and Gaunt lamenting the failings of Richard's conduct as King. When Richard himself enters (line 69), Gaunt rebukes him for: submitting himself to the evil influence of flatterers; shaming the noble blood of Edward III and killing his descendants; and leasing out his land in return for money. Almost immediately after Gaunt has left the stage (line 138) news is brought of his death. Triumphantly, Richard immediately plans to seize his wealth to finance his Irish campaign. York, Gaunt's brother and now 'the last of noble Edward's sons' (line 171), endeavours to dissuade the King from thus depriving Henry Bolingbroke of his inheritance. He points out that Richard himself holds his throne by the laws of inheritance: to deny Henry his birthright is to deny his own title to the crown and to undermine the very foundations of society. York also foretells terrible consequences if Richard goes ahead with his scheme. Richard, however, disregards York and leaves determined to set out for Ireland the next day, making York Governor of England in his absence. After the King has left, three noblemen (Northumberland, Willoughby and Ross) remain on stage and discuss the wrongs which they and England have endured under Richard. After some persuasion, Northumberland reveals that Henry is ready to sail from France with an invasion force, and that he is only waiting for Richard to leave for Ireland before setting out. The three agree to meet him at the port of Ravenspurgh.

> This is a pivotal scene in the play's structure. It concludes the first movement of the drama and begins the second, Richard's downfall (see Plot & Structure). It is crucial to the action as it draws together and confirms everything that has been learned about Richard as King and shows him making a decision (to seize Gaunt's wealth) which will be the immediate cause of the loss of his throne. This is Richard's last appearance as an unchallenged king: after he exits

(line 223), he is not seen again until the balance of power has shifted decisively to Henry, in III.2.

The pace of this scene begins to create an impression of irresistible momentum as its events seem to move very fast and to occur immediately after Henry's banishment. In fact, Shakespeare has telescoped time to achieve this effect. Henry was banished in September 1398; Gaunt died in February 1399; Richard did not leave for Ireland until three months later, in May 1399; and Henry landed in July. There is no sense of this passage of time in the play. Indeed, it all happens too quickly to be realistic: it is only in this scene that Richard decides to deny Henry his rights, so Henry could not possibly know already that he has been disinherited; and yet, it seems, he has already organised an invasion force. But dramatically it gives the impression that events are now taking control and that Richard is helpless to prevent them.

As yet it is not clear just what Henry hopes to gain by invading England: there is only a general feeling that he is coming to right his own, and perhaps England's, wrongs. The decision of the three nobles and the indications we had in I.4 of popular support for Henry prepare us to expect that he will not be resisted and that Richard will quickly be deserted by any followers. So begins the King's fall.

There is no clue for the opening of this scene in Shakespeare's sources, nor for the dignity, wisdom and nobility he gives to Gaunt, whose 'England' speech (lines 31–68) is entirely Shakespeare's invention (see Shakespeare's Use of Sources). It is not, however, difficult to see why Shakespeare chose to introduce the incident. The scene begins by stressing Richard's youthful folly more strongly than has yet been done by having the old and experienced noble princes, York and Gaunt, speak despairingly of him. In Gaunt's very famous prophetic speech there is a superb expression of patriotic devotion to the England which Richard threatens to destroy. In fact, Shakespeare conveys in these lines far more than one man's particular affection for his country: the speech celebrates the patriotic fervour which runs through all the history plays and gives a moving vision of that England which, finally, triumphs in the Tudors over all the wars and treacheries which follow Richard's death. Hearing it, the Elizabethans would hear *their* England described. Particularly, the speech highlights Richard's negligence in failing to rule such a kingdom well.

s.d. **Duke of York** Edmund of Langley (1341–1402), fifth son of Edward III and so Gaunt's brother, Aumerle's father and uncle to Richard and Henry: his descendants (the Yorkists) were to fight Gaunt's descendants (the Lancastrians) for the English crown in the Wars of the Roses
Earl of Northumberland Sir Henry Percy (1342–1408), father of Harry Percy (the Hotspur of *Henry IV Part 1*)

2 **unstaid** uncontrolled, unrestrained

10 **glose** flatter

13 **As the last taste of sweets, is sweetest last** either 'as the final taste of a sweet thing is sweetest because it is last' or 'the final taste of a sweet thing is sweetest because, being the last, it lingers longest'

19 **Lascivious metres** wanton verse

21 **Italy** Elizabethan writers habitually attributed decadent, corrupt and evil practices to Italy

22 **tardy-apish** York means that the English imitate a fashion when it is already out of date

24 **vanity** silly, inconsequential thing

28 **Where will doth mutiny with wit's regard** when the will overrules the understanding

30 **'Tis breath thou lackest, and that breath wilt thou lose** to advise Richard is a waste of breath, and Gaunt has little enough to spare both because, as he is ill, he has difficulty breathing and is short of breath, and because, as he is dying, he has only a few more breaths to draw

31 **Methinks I am a prophet new-inspired** the idea that, in their dying moments, men might become prophetic, was common (see also lines 5–6)

32 **expiring** dying, but the pun on 'breath' continues: by breathing in ('inspiring') Gaunt has gained breath which he now breathes out ('expires') in what follows

33 **riot** wasteful and extravagant way of life

36 **betimes** 'soon', and, at the end of the line, 'early in the day'

38-9 **Light ... means** a frivolous way of life, like a gluttonous cormorant consuming everything (the cormorant swallows fish whole)

41 **this seat of Mars** as Mars was the Roman god of war, the suggestion is that England is famous for military bravery

42 **Eden** the paradise in which, according to the Bible, the first man and woman, Adam and Eve, lived until their fall from God's favour

demi-paradise one of two paradises (rather than half a paradise), the other being in Eden

44 **infection** evil foreign influences

49 **envy** hatred, hostility

52 **Feared by their breed** inspiring fear by the nobility of their breeding

by their birth on account of their noble birth

54 **For Christian service and true chivalry** this line enlarges on 'deeds' in line 53, and so the phrase 'as far from home' (line 53) would more naturally follow it: their deeds of Christian service (that is, the Crusades) and chivalry are renowned as far from home as is Christ's tomb (line 55)

55 **sepulchre** the tomb in which, according to the Bible, Christ was laid after the Crucifixion and from which he rose from the dead

stubborn Jewry the Jews were held to be stubborn for refusing to be converted to Christianity

56 **the world's ransom** Christians believe Christ died for the sins of the whole world – that is, his death frees human beings from the punishment due to their sin, as the payment of a ransom frees a captive taken in war

Mary's son Christ

60 **pelting** paltry, insignificant

64 **inky blots and rotten parchment bonds** the blank charters mentioned in I.4.48

s.d. **Queen Isabel** Richard married his second wife, Isàbella (1389–1409), daughter of Charles V of France, in 1396, when she was only eight years old, but in Shakespeare's play she is a mature woman

70 **raged** it seems rather pointless to say that young horses 'rage the more' when they are 'raged': some editors therefore change 'raged' to 'rein'd', which makes sense (young horses, if restrained, get angrier) and fits with York's argument that the young king is best not rebuked

75 **tedious fast** painful and long fast

77 **watched** three senses mingle here: looked at (England's state), been kept awake (by worry) and kept a vigil

78 **Watching** sleeplessness

79–80 **The pleasure ... looks** as Gaunt is denied the pleasure of his son Henry, he abstains (or fasts) from what most fathers enjoy

83 **inherits** possesses

84 **nicely** both subtly and foolishly

86 **kill my name in me** by banishing his heir, in whom his name would live after his death; Gaunt does not know that Richard intends to kill his name completely by denying Henry his inheritance

93 **he that made me** God

94 **Ill in myself to see, and in thee seeing ill** it makes me ill to see you, and in you I see evil

97 **careless patient** careless as a patient

99 **those 'physicians' that first wounded thee** Gaunt refers to Richard's circle of favourites, the 'flatterers' of line 100

101 **compass** circumference

102 **verge** area (strictly, the area surrounding a court)

104 **grandsire** Edward III

105 **son's son** Richard

sons Gloucester and Gaunt

106 **forth** out of

107 **possessed** in possession of (your kingdom)

108 **possessed** possessed by follies and passions

109 **regent** ruler

111 **But for thy world enjoying but this land** but as you enjoy only this land (and not the whole world) as your kingdom

114 **Thy state of law is bondslave to the law** as Richard has let out his land for money he is no longer its king, the source of law, but a landlord who is subject, like any other, to the common laws of the land

119 **native** natural

121 **great Edward's son** Edward the Black Prince, Edward III's son and Richard's father

122 **roundly** bluntly or glibly; either sense may be intended

123 **Should run thy head from thy unreverent shoulders** were Gaunt not of royal blood his words would deserve execution as punishment

124 **my brother Edward** the Black Prince

125 **his father Edward** Edward III

126 **pelican** the mother pelican was thought to feed her young with blood from a self-inflicted wound

127 **tapped out** let out

129 **fair befall** may good come to

139 **sullens** sulks

144 **Harry** Henry Bolingbroke

145 **As Hereford's love, so his** York has asserted that Gaunt loves Richard as dearly as he loves his own son, Henry, which Richard deliberately takes to mean that Gaunt's feeling for him is no warmer than is Henry's

154 **His time is spent, our pilgrimage must be** his life is over, ours is still before us

156 **rug-headed kerns** long-haired Irish soldiers

157–8 **where ... live** according to legend, St Patrick, patron saint of Ireland, drove all snakes from the island

159 **charge** expenditure

161 **plate** gold and silver plates, cups and dishes

166 **Gaunt's rebukes** the rebukes given to Gaunt by Richard (not vice versa) **private wrongs** wrongs suffered by ordinary citizens

167–8 **Nor ... marriage** Richard had prevented Henry's intended marriage, as Holinshed (see Shakespeare's Use of Sources) records

177 **Accomplished with the number of thy hours** when he was your age

179–81 **His noble head ... won** a reference to the fact that, unlike his father, Richard has had no military successes (which would have brought tribute, taxes and ransoms into the treasury)

190 **royalties** rights granted by the King, titles

196 **His charters and his customary rights** agreements and traditional laws of inheritance

202–4 **Call in ... livery** upon a nobleman's death his lands became the property of the King until the heir proved himself entitled to succeed and to be of age: the 'letters patents' were issued by the King to allow the prospective inheritor to have lawyers ('attorneys general') go through the legal process of inheriting his father's lands and titles ('sue / His livery'); by revoking them ('Call in') Richard would prevent Henry from becoming Duke of Lancaster and would himself remain in control of the Lancastrian wealth

204 **deny his offered homage** an heir received his inheritance on condition he made an act of homage to the King: to refuse ('deny') homage from Henry would thus be to refuse him his inheritance

207–8 **those thoughts ... think** thoughts of disobedience and rebellion unbecoming a loyal subject

213–14 **But ... good** we may be sure ('understood') that the consequences ('events') of bad actions ('courses') can never be ('fall out') good

215 **Earl of Wiltshire** William le Scrope (?1351–99), Richard's treasurer. He is executed with Bushy and Green at Bristol (III.2.122–42), but he does not appear in the play

216 **Ely House** where Richard now is and this scene is set (see I.4.58)

218 **time I trow** high time I believe

219 **in absence of ourself** while I am away

228 **great** full of emotion

229 **liberal** free, unrestrained (Ross is afraid to speak his mind lest his words be reported to Richard)

243 **Merely in** simply out of

246 **pilled** robbed, plundered

250 **blanks, benevolences** blank charters (see I.4.48) and forced loans
     wot know

251 **this** the money raised by the loans and other devices

253 **compromise** a compromise peace treaty

265 **sore** dangerously

266 **strike** take down sail (that is, take precautions) with a pun on 'strike' in the sense of 'strike' or 'fight back'
     securely carelessly, over-confidently

269 **suffering** tolerating

270 **hollow eyes** the eye-sockets of a skull

275 **are but thyself** are one with you, agree with you

277 **Le Port Blanc** a port on the French coast of Brittany (the 'Brittaine' of line 278)

279–85 **Rainold Lord Cobham ... Duke of Brittaine** who these figures were matters less to an audience than the impression of large-scale support for Henry which the list creates; they are all taken direct from Holinshed (see Shakespeare's Use of Sources) and none appears in the play

281 **broke** escaped

287 **expedience** speed

288 **touch** land on

292 **Imp** repair with new feathers (a term used in falconry)

293 **broking pawn** pawn-brokers, money-lenders

296 **Ravenspurgh** a port in England on the river Humber

300 **Hold out my horse** if my horse can hold out (that is, riding at speed)

SCENE 2   **When, upon Richard's departure for Ireland, Henry lands in England, the regent York admits he will be unable to mount effective resistance and Richard's friends flee**

The Queen, saddened by her parting from Richard, who has now left for Ireland, is troubled by fears for the future, when news is brought that Henry, who had only been waiting for Richard's departure (II.1.289–90), has now landed in England. The Duke of York, regent in Richard's absence, dismayed by news of the death of his sister-in-law and troubled by his divided loyalties (to Richard and to Henry), confesses himself unable effectively to confront Henry. The scene ends with Richard's close counsellors and friends fleeing to save their lives.

This short scene makes a significant contribution to the play in the way it affects our view of Richard and his fortunes:

• The Queen is naturally sad at being parted from Richard, but her additional struggle with a 'nameless woe' (line 40), an ominous fear for the future, creates an air of foreboding and dread just as news arrives that Henry Bolingbroke has landed.

• In showing the Queen's love and concern for Richard, the scene begins the very process whereby, after Richard's rather treacherous dealings in I.4 and II.1, sympathy is gradually generated for him – to the Queen he is a wronged man, not a scheming tyrant.

• The death of the Duchess of Gloucester, York's sister-in-law, deepens the atmosphere of gloom, but, more significantly, it stresses the helplessness of York. He is Governor of England in Richard's absence, but he has little hope of resisting Henry. He had hoped to ask his sister-in-law for money (lines 90–2) but her death prevents this and, by adding to his sorrow, only makes him more perplexed. He is stunned: 'I know not what to do' (line 100). York had shown himself a mild man when he had tried to dissuade Gaunt from speaking out in II.1; it now appears he is quite unfit to protect Richard's interests. Not only is he impractical, but he has much sympathy for Henry (lines 109–15). Already it seems Richard's position is virtually hopeless.

• This impression is confirmed at the end of the scene, when Richard's favourites desert York (and thus Richard's cause) to save their lives. Convinced York's position is hopeless, they expect never to meet again. Nobles have left Richard; the common people feel no affection for him (line 88); York is helpless; and now Richard's dearest friends flee. Clearly, the coming of Henry has put all in disarray and there is no one to stop him (lines 144–6).

In these various respects, the scene confirms the **tragic** turn of events hinted at in II.1.

8 **Save bidding farewell to** unless it is that I have said goodbye to

14 **Each substance of a grief hath twenty shadows** for each real cause of sorrow there are twenty imaginary ones

18 **perspectives** two senses are used here: a glass so cut that it reflects many images (the comparison in lines 16–17); and a picture so designed that it appears distorted unless viewed from a special and awkward angle (the comparison of lines 18–20)

20 **Distinguish form** show clear shapes

21 **Looking awry upon your lord's departure** if Bushy were still thinking of the second kind of 'perspective' (see line 18) this would give a true picture; but as he is arguing that the Queen sees more causes of sorrow than there actually are (line 22), he appears to have returned to the comparison with the first kind of 'perspective'. The passage is confusing, but the main point to grasp is the distinction between real and imaginary causes of sorrow

22 **Find** finds ('your sweet majesty' of line 20 is the subject)

23 **Which looked on as it is** which shapes of grief, looked on as they are, are

27 **Which for things true weeps things imaginary** which, instead of weeping because of true things, weeps for imaginary ones

31 **though on thinking on no thought I think** though I am thinking on nothing melancholy ('thought')

33 **conceit** imagination, fancy (Bushy implies that it is nothing *more* than imaginary, hence the Queen's reply in line 34)

34 **nothing less** anything but

35–40 **Mine is not so ... I wot** the wordplay now becomes very intricate. This passage might be paraphrased as follows: My grief is not mere fancy, for either an imaginary cause of sorrow ('nothing', line 36) has resulted in ('begot') my real sorrow ('something grief'), or there is an actual cause of grief ('something', line 37) which, though I do not know what it is, would

justify the sorrow ('nothing') which I feel ('grieve') – if so, it is mine
because I feel it, even though its cause as yet belongs elsewhere
(line 38) – I cannot give a name to what is not yet known: 'nameless
woe' would, I suppose, be the best way to describe it

44 **his haste good hope** in his haste lies good hope

46 **retired his power** brought back his armed forces

58 **Earl of Worcester** Sir Thomas Percy (?1344–1403), brother of
Northumberland; he does not appear in this play but has a significant part
in *Henry IV Part 1*

59 **staff** the symbol of Thomas Percy's office of steward of the royal household

64 **prodigy** unnatural thing, monstrous child

69 **cozening** cheating, deceitful

72 **lingers in extremity** prolongs as long as possible

74 **signs of war about his agèd neck** York wears a piece of neck armour

79 **crosses** frustrations, troubles

80 **far off** what lies far away (that is, Ireland)

86 **your son** Aumerle, who has gone to Ireland with Richard

90 **Pleshey** Gloucester's country house (I.2.66)

sister Gloucester sister-in-law, the Duchess of Gloucester

96 **knave** fellow (with no contemptuous overtone)

98 **God for his mercy** a common exclamation

101 **So my untruth had not provoked him to it** as long as my loyalty was not the
cause

102 **my brother** Gloucester

103 **posts** messengers

105 **sister – cousin, I would say** York addresses the Queen, his cousin or
kinswoman (by her marriage to Richard), but the death of the Duchess
is uppermost in his mind and so, thinking of her, he says 'sister' by
mistake

111 **Never believe me** do not believe me if I say it

120 **uneven** confused

122–3 **The wind ... returns** the wind is in the right direction to blow ships to
Ireland, but not from it

127 **Is near** occasions

136 **office** service

141 **presages** fears for the future

143 **thrives to beat** succeeds in driving

SCENE 3   **Henry, meeting no opposition, gathers support as he marches through England**

Henry is making his way through Gloucestershire in the company of Northumberland (who had gone to meet him at Ravenspurgh at the end of II.1). As he does so, he meets no opposition and is joined by a steady succession of supporters – Harry Percy, Ross and Willoughby. When he comes to Berkeley Castle, held by York, there is still no opposition. Henry claims that he has come only to secure his rights as Duke of Lancaster (and we know that York has much sympathy for the justice of his claim – see II.1.189–99, II.2.111–15). York, while he cannot condone Henry's breaking of the law in returning to England with an army, admits he has no power to stop him, and so withdraws from the contest, claiming to be neutral. Nevertheless, he invites Henry and his entourage to spend the night at his castle, and we learn that Henry intends to go on to Bristol, where two of Richard's favourites are in hiding.

What is made clear in this scene is the *ease* of the invasion: Henry rides through England not like an outlaw and rebel but like a hero welcomed by all he meets. Dramatically this confirms the impression that, with no support, Richard is doomed. The turning of fortune's wheel, which began at the end of II.1 and was so evident in II.2, is accelerating.

10 **In Ross and Willoughby** by Ross and Willoughby
11 **beguiled** eased
12 **process** progress
s.d. **Harry Percy** the Earl of Northumberland's son, Sir Henry Percy (1364–1403), who, as Hotspur, plays an important role in the rebellion of the Percys against Henry covered in *Henry IV Part 1*. The 'boy' of line 36 and his protestations of youth in line 42 suggest that Shakespeare's character is younger than the historical Hotspur, who was in fact three years older than Henry Bolingbroke
22 **whencesoever** wherever he is
44 **more approvèd** more fully demonstrated
45 **gentle** noble
47 **As in a soul remembering** as in having a heart which remembers
49 **It shall be still thy true love's recompense** it shall constantly ('still') reward ('recompense') your true love

51 **stir** preparation

61 **unfelt** unfelt by those he would thank, since he is not yet able to give them any positive reward

65 **Evermore thank's the exchequer of the poor** thanks are always what the poor offer

67 **Stands for my bounty** must take the place of my generosity

70 **'Lancaster'** now that Gaunt is dead, Henry is rightfully Duke of Lancaster, a title which takes precedence over Duke of Hereford

75 **raze** take away

79 **absent time** time when the King is absent

80 **self-borne** borne in your own interest (and not the King's)

91 **more 'why'** more questions

103 **palsy** a form of paralysis, often suffered by the aged

113 **for Lancaster** to claim the rights of the Duke of Lancaster

115 **indifferent** impartial

127 **To rouse his wrongs and chase them to the bay** the line uses metaphors from hunting: to 'rouse' is to startle from hiding; the 'bay' is the quarry's last stand after the chase before being killed. The sense is thus 'to seek out his wrongdoers and pursue them until they are caught'

133 **I challenge law** what I demand is in the name of the law

137 **It stands your grace upon** it is up to your grace

138 **endowments** possessions

142 **kind** way

143 **Be his own carver** an expression meaning 'help yourself', 'decide for yourself' (the carver of a joint of meat at table would serve himself)

144 **find out right with wrong** gain the right by doing wrong

152 **mend** prevent

155 **attach** arrest

158 **neuter** neutral

164 **Bagot** Bagot had gone to Ireland (II.2.140), Bushy and Green to Bristol (II.2.134, 136); Shakespeare seems to have confused Bagot with Green

165 **caterpillars** parasites

SCENE 4   **The Welsh forces awaiting Richard's return disband**

Frustrated by the delay in Richard's return from Ireland, and hearing rumours that he is in fact dead, the Welsh forces gathered to support him disband. Discouraged by this turn of events, the Earl of Salisbury foresees Richard's overthrow.

This brief scene achieves three effects: it gives the impression of a lapse of time between II.3 and III.1, during which Henry can travel from Berkeley Castle to Bristol; it intensifies our sense of Richard's predicament by showing yet again supporters deserting him; and it deepens the mood of ominous foreboding by adding to the prophecies of doom introduced by Gaunt and York in II.1 and continued by the Queen in II.2 – Salisbury's final speech seems to set the seal on Richard's fate.

s.d. **Earl of Salisbury** John Montagu (1350–1400) who, remaining faithful to Richard, takes part in the plot treated in Act V

Welsh Captain in Holinshed (see Shakespeare's Use of Sources) named as Owen Glendower (?1359–?1416), who took a prominent part in the rebellion against Henry treated in the *Henry IV* plays

6 **reposeth** places

8 **bay trees** the bay is an evergreen tree whose leaves were used to make medicine; in art it is a **symbol** of victory and immortality, so its withering suggests defeat and death

9 **meteors** falling stars

fixèd stars in Renaissance cosmology the stars were thought to be fixed in their position around the earth

10 **The pale-faced moon looks bloody on the earth** the stars and planets were thought to exert an influence on the affairs of human beings, so 'looks' carries two senses: the pale moon appears blood red from the earth; and the pale moon exerts a bloody (disastrous) influence over the earth

22 **Witnessing** suggesting

ACT III

SCENE 1   **Arriving at Bristol Castle, Henry has Bushy and Green executed**

Henry has come to Bristol Castle (as he planned, II.3.163–4) and, having captured Bushy and Green (who had fled there, II.2.134, 136), has them immediately executed. He justifies this by charging them with separating the King from the Queen; misrepresenting him to the King; and wronging him by misusing his lands and destroying the symbols of his nobility.

Shakespeare pays no attention to how Henry took Bristol Castle or captured Bushy and Green; the castle, and the men, are simply in his power when the scene opens. Practical action and the overcoming of opposition are written out of the play. Shakespeare thus continues to suggest that Henry's progress is effortless: he seems to have to do nothing at all.

4 **too much urging** too much insisting on

7 **unfold** reveal, make known

10 **clean** completely

11 **in manner** in a manner of speaking

sinful hours the many hours during which they kept Richard from Isabel by involving him in extravagant pleasures. There may be a suggestion of homosexuality here, but if so, it is not developed

12 **divorce** separation

13 **Broke the possession of a royal bed** broke the royal union both enjoyed

18 **misinterpret** misunderstand

22 **signories** estates

23 **Disparked** used for purposes other than the (noble) business of keeping game for hunting

24 **From my own windows torn my household coat** broken my windows, on which was painted my heraldic coat of arms

25 **imprese** heraldic device, badge

sign family symbol

37 **intreated** treated

38 **commends** wishes

43 **Glendower** Henry does not yet know that the Welsh army has disbanded. Whether Shakespeare identified Glendower with the Welsh Captain of II.4 is not clear

SCENE 2   **Richard returns from Ireland and, receiving a succession of bad news, despairs of his situation**

Richard lands at Barkloughly and is overjoyed to be back in his kingdom. He beseeches the earth itself to help him against the rebels. The Bishop of Carlisle assures Richard that God can keep him King, but adds that men should exert themselves to bring about God's will. Aumerle more pointedly says that they must make plans to deal with Henry. Richard rejects this as advice unworthy of a king: he is idealistically (and impractically) confident in the power of his mere kingly presence to win support and to shame Henry and his followers into submission.

A succession of three disappointments shatters Richard's confidence. First, Salisbury arrives with the news that the Welsh army has disbanded (as we saw in II.4). Immediately Richard is plunged into despair, but he revives upon recalling that he is still the King and that this is worth 'twenty thousand' men (line 85). But then Sir Stephen Scroop arrives and paints a dismal picture of an entire kingdom in arms against its king, concluding with the news that Richard's favourites have been executed (as we saw in the previous scene). Richard's despair this time is deeper: in one of Shakespeare's most famous speeches (lines 144–77) he dwells on death and the futility of kingly splendour. However, he revives again when Aumerle reminds him that there is still his father York with his army. However, Scroop then reluctantly admits that even York has defected to Henry. Richard now refuses all comfort. As far as he is concerned, the situation is hopeless. He discharges his soldiers and withdraws to Flint Castle, abandoning the contest without a fight. His sun has set: it is now 'Bolingbroke's fair day' (line 218).

> This is in many respects the pivotal scene of the play: though no battle has been fought, and Richard's submission to Henry and deposition are yet to come, power now irrevocably slips from him. This is the first time that Richard has been on stage since he left for Ireland in II.1. In the intervening scenes, the balance of power has shifted decisively to Henry who, without a struggle, has become effective ruler of all England. Of this the audience is fully aware, but Richard returns ignorant of how decisively his position has changed. He has a far weaker grasp of his true situation than the audience. There is hence a tragic **irony** throughout the scene as Richard is disabused of his misconceptions and is brought to recognise what the audience already knows, the true state of things.

> In the process, new qualities in Richard begin to emerge. He shows himself to be capable of affecting poetic expression, but he also

shows himself to be emotionally unstable and incapable of resolute
action. Rather than a sordid tyrant reaping his just rewards, the
scene depicts a sensitive, self-pitying character struggling with
adversity, see-sawing between hope and despair.

s.d. **Bishop of Carlisle** Thomas Merke (died 1409), one of Richard's staunchest
supporters

1 **Barkloughly** modern-day Harlech, in Wales

11 **And do thee favours with my royal hands** Richard touches the earth with his
hand (line 6), and to be touched by a royal hand is a privilege

13 **sweets** good things harvested from the earth

14 **venom** it was thought that spiders sucked up poison from the earth

15 **toads** thought to be poisonous

16 **treacherous feet** the rebels

21 **double tongue** the forked tongue of the adder in line 20

23 **my senseless conjuration** my solemn appeal to things without sense

31 **And we will not** we would fail to keep you king (by failing to take the
necessary action)

34 **security** overconfidence

37 **searching eye** the sun: Richard compares his absence in Ireland to the
absence of the sun at night when it lights the earth elsewhere

42 **He** the sun: Richard's suggestion in the following lines is that just as
criminals who prefer to act under cover of darkness (lines 39–40) flee
when the sun comes up, so his mere presence will frighten the rebels into
submission

49 **with the Antipodes** with (the people who live on) the opposite side of the
earth: Richard has, of course, only been to Ireland, but he continues the
comparison of his absence to that of the sun

53 **self-affrighted** self-condemned

55 **balm** the oil with which a king is consecrated at his coronation

57 **The deputy elected by the Lord** the line refers to the belief, crucial to
Richard's thinking, that a king is chosen for his sacred office by God, and
so is answerable only to God

59 **shrewd** harmful, malicious

crown Shakespeare puns on the fact that 'crown' and 'angel' (line 61) were
both types of coin

81 **blot** stain (in that he has been deserted by the Welsh) *s.d.* **Scroop** Sir Stephen Scroop (died 1408), one of the few who remained faithful to Richard even after his arrest (not the Earl of Wiltshire, see p. 36 of this Note)

91 **betide** may (more health and happiness) come to

109 **his limits** its proper bounds

114 **female** womanish (here implying 'weak')

116 **beadsmen** men paid to pray for others

117 **double-fatal** as the yew tree is poisonous and its wood was used for making bows it was a double cause of death

118 **distaff-women** women who spin thread

manage wield

bills weapons with long wooden handles and axes' heads

122–3 **Earl of Wiltshire ... Bagot ... Bushy ... Green** Bagot was not executed at Bristol, nor had Shakespeare included him amongst those killed in III.1 (although he had mistakenly placed Bagot there in II.3.163–4). Yet before Richard knows this (he is informed at lines 141–2) he exclaims against only *three* 'Judases' in line 132, after having named *four* men here; similarly Aumerle, for no clear reason, names only three of the four at line 141. This looks like a simple slip on Shakespeare's part

125 **Measure our confines** walk over our lands

peaceful unopposed

132 **Judas** the disciple who betrayed Jesus (Luke 22:47–8)

135 **property** quality

138 **With heads and not with hands** not by shaking Henry's hand but by sacrificing their heads

153 **model** the mound raised over a grave

154 **paste and cover** an **image** taken from a pie crust, since this was sometimes called a 'coffin'

162 **antic** jester: death was often pictured as a skeleton grinning at his victims

163 **Scoffing his state** mocking his (the King's) worldly status

166 **self** of himself (an adjective governing 'conceit')

168 **humoured thus** this could mean either 'death having been thus entertained for a while by this spectacle of men pretending to be powerful', or 'the King having been thus lulled for a while by enjoying his pomp'

171 **Cover your heads** Richard directs his followers no longer to show him the marks of respect due to a king (in the presence of whom heads would ordinarily be uncovered)

174 **For you have but mistook me all this while** both because Richard is not the mighty king he has seemed to be (death is the real ruler) and because he is a man like any other

179 **But presently prevent the ways to wail** but stop the cause of grief by prompt action

184–5 **And fight ... breath** to die fighting is to destroy death's power by refusing to be in awe of him, whereas to fear to die is to be the slave of death

187 **learn to make a body of a limb** learn to make his small force serve for the army you should have

190 **overblown** passed

212 **ear** plough

grow literally 'cultivate', but in terms of the **image**, also 'prosper'

SCENE 3 　At Flint Castle Richard, confronted by Henry and his army, puts up no resistance and is conveyed to London

Reporting to Henry that Richard is nearby, Northumberland neglects to call him 'King Richard', and is rebuked by York, who voices the first clear suspicion in the play that Henry is after more than simply his rights as Duke of Lancaster (lines 16–17). Nevertheless Henry, learning that Richard is in Flint Castle, sends Northumberland as his messenger to Richard to proclaim that this *is* all he seeks – his rights as duke, with the repeal of his banishment. Richard appears on the castle battlements (that is, on the balcony over the stage) and speaks with all the regal dignity and apparent confidence of which he is capable. Northumberland's address (lines 101–20) details Henry's demands and explains that Henry will submit and disband his army if they are granted. The words sound well, but Northumberland also stresses (as Henry had instructed, lines 42–4) Henry's military superiority and his willingness to fight to gain what he wants. In other words, Richard has no choice. This the King recognises: he immediately agrees to all Henry's terms, though he is ashamed to do so and does not believe for a moment that Henry will be satisfied with what he has asked for. Richard is in no doubt that Henry aims at the crown, and is fully aware that he is in the power of 'King Bolingbroke' (line 173). He descends to meet Henry and agrees to go to London.

In this scene the long-anticipated confrontation between Henry and Richard (which occurred in August 1399) finally comes about. However, it does so in a curious way. In Holinshed (see Shakespeare's Use of Sources), Northumberland meets Richard in Wales, persuades him to set out to meet Henry with a promise of safe conduct, and then has him ambushed and taken as a prisoner to Flint Castle, where Henry comes to him. In other words, Henry contrives to have Richard captured. In this scene, however, Henry takes no such steps. He and his followers are unaware that Richard is in Flint Castle, and they are most surprised when they find out (lines 20–30). The effect of Shakespeare's change is once again to stress the ease with which Henry succeeds: he stumbles upon the King, having planned nothing. Fate is clearly on his side.

Though the scene ends with Henry having said nothing about his plans, there can now be little doubt that Richard's interpretation of them is correct and that he will be deposed.

1 **So that by this intelligence we learn** the scene begins in mid-conversation. The 'intelligence' (information) has presumably come in the form of a letter which Henry is reading

2 **Welshmen** in III.1.43 Henry had been planning to fight the Welsh; he has now learned what occurred in II.4

14 **For taking so the head** both for acting impetuously (in forgetting courtesy) and for depriving the King of his title
your whole head's length by executing you

20 **this castle** Flint Castle (see lines 21–5 and III.2.209)

31 **Noble lord** Northumberland

32 **rude ribs** rough walls

33 **brazen** brass
breath of parley trumpet call to invite an opponent to negotiations

48 **stooping duty** kneeling

53 **appointments** equipment

56–7 **Of fire ... heaven** it was believed that thunder was caused by the meeting of the elements of fire (lightning) and water (rain)

58 **Be he the fire, I'll be the yielding water** fire was the primary of the four elements (earth, air, fire and water), so Henry appears to be saying that he is willing for Richard to be superior, that is, king

69 **eagle** the first among (king of) birds and so a royal **symbol**

76 **awful** in awe, respectful

76 **duty** the kneeling required of a dutiful subject

87 **pestilence** Richard is probably recalling the plagues God sent against the Egyptians on behalf of Moses and the Israelites (Exodus 8:1–11:10)

88 **unbegot** not yet conceived

94 **The purple testament of bleeding war** will which bequeaths bloody war

96 **crowns** heads

97 **Shall ill become the flower of England's face** both the faces of English youth and the face of England, equally despoiled by bloody decapitation

100 **pastor's** shepherd's; there is also a hint of the religious sense of priest

102 **civil and uncivil arms** weapons used in civil war barbarously

108 **one most gracious head** namely, Edward III's

117 **barbèd** armoured

136 **sooth** appeasement

140 **scope** room

141 **scope** permission

146 **A** in

147 **beads** a rosary, used by Roman Catholics to assist the memory in prayer

150 **figured** ornamented, engraved

151 **palmer** pilgrim

152 **carvèd saints** carved wooden models of saints

156 **trade** traffic

159 **buried once** once buried

162 **lodge** beat down

165 **pretty match** game

168 **and therein laid there lies** the sense requires a break after 'laid' – the meaning is: 'and therein are we laid; our epitaph might be "There lies ..."' '

173–4 **Will ... die?** Richard already sees that his life is in danger when he poses this ironic question, which must be answered 'yes' whatever Henry intends

176 **base-court** lower courtyard on ground level

178 **Phaethon** in Greek myth the son of the sun god Apollo, who, taking his father's sun chariot, was unable to control it and was killed by a thunderbolt from Zeus to prevent him from colliding with the earth

179 **jades** contemptuous term for horses

180 **base-court** Richard here plays on the other sense of 'base', meaning despicable, ignoble

183 **mounting** climbing (the lark sings as it ascends)

195 **Thus** Richard presumably gestures to the crown on his head

198 **redoubted** dreaded, feared

203 **but want their remedies** but cannot remedy the cause of weeping

SCENE 4   **The Queen learns that Richard is in Henry's power and resolves to travel to London**

Walking in a garden, Queen Isabel, ignorant of what has become of Richard, wishes she might be entertained to take her mind off her worries, but she cannot be satisfied with any of her ladies' suggestions. When the gardeners enter, she retires to overhear their conversation. As she had expected, they talk of public affairs. The news that Richard is now in Henry's power wrings from the Queen a cry of disbelief. The scene ends as she resolves to travel to London herself.

> This is the second of the three scenes (the others are II.2 and V.1) in which Shakespeare, departing from his sources, concentrates upon the Queen (who is portrayed as a mature woman to gain his effect). Her love and concern for Richard invite the audience to share in her sympathetic view of him and his fate. It is a private scene, very different in tone and setting from the events of public significance which precede and follow it. In this respect, it offers a contrast to, and a pause in, the developing **tragic** action of the play, which resumes in the next scene, IV.1; but it is also a **choric** scene of commentary upon that action.

> From II.2.116–7, III.1.36 and line 70 of this scene, the location can be identified as the Duke of York's garden, but an audience could hardly be expected to work this out: the fact that it is a garden (line 1), far from the events of III.2–3, and after Richard has set out for London, is what matters. This retreat, removed from political rivalries and schemes, allows events to be viewed from a perspective very different to that of those directly involved.

> In the gardeners' conversation Shakespeare develops in detail the comparison of the state of England under Richard to an unweeded and untended garden. This **simile** has been used before in the play (II.3.165–6), and was a common one with writers of Shakespeare's time, especially **satirists** and commentators on state events. It suggests that, for all the sorrow which the plight of the man arouses

in the Queen, by his negligence as King, Richard is himself ultimately responsible for his downfall.

4 **rubs** difficulty (a technical term in the game of bowls for something which obstructs the 'wood' or bowl)

5 **bias** a wood is weighted on one side so that it rolls in a curve: to run 'against the bias' is to go in a direction other than the one the wood would naturally take, and so the Queen means that her fortune is going badly

7 **keep ... measure** 'follow the steps of a dance' and 'keep time'

8 **measure** limit

15 **altogether had** possessed completely

22-3 **And I ... thee** and if my troubles were only such as weeping could make better, then I would sing for joy and have no need to ask you to weep for me

26 **My wretchedness unto a row of pins** I will bet my sadness against a row of pins – that is, something very great against something very small, implying she is confident that they will 'talk of state' (line 27)

28 **Against a change** when they expect a change

Woe is forerun with woe sad events are preceded by foreseeing and lamenting them

31 **Stoop with oppression of their prodigal weight** 'prodigal' means both 'excessive' and 'wastefully extravagant', so the line suggests a father literally bowed down with the weight of his children and **metaphorically** bowed down with the cares their extravagance causes him

38 **noisome** harmful

40 **in the compass of a pale** within the limits of a fence

42 **as in a model** perfectly

firm estate stable administration of government

43 **sea-wallèd garden** England (the sea being the 'wall' or 'moat defensive' of Gaunt's speech, II.1.46–9)

46 **knots** flower-beds

47 **caterpillars** the word Henry used of Richard's favourites in II.3.165

56 **dressed** cultivated

57 **at time of year** at the appropriate season

59 **overproud** too luxuriant, too fruitful

60 **confound** destroy

68 **Depressed** brought low

Act III continued

72 **O, I am pressed to death through want of speaking!** the Queen uses a legal **metaphor**: a person charged with a crime who refused to plead either 'guilty' or 'not guilty' (that is, who remained silent, as the Queen has done while listening to this conversation) was 'pressed' with weights until either they spoke and made a plea or died (a man might prefer to die since, if he entered a plea and were found guilty, his heir could not inherit his estate)

73 **old Adam** Adam was a gardener in Eden (Genesis 2:15); he is called 'old' to distinguish him from the 'new Adam', Christ

75 **serpent** the serpent tempted Eve to eat the forbidden fruit in Eden and so caused the 'Fall of cursèd man' (line 76) from happiness (Genesis 3) **suggested** tempted

79 **Divine** prophesy

86 **vanities** follies and, especially, Richard's favourites

93 **embassage** message

95 **serve me** deliver your message to me

105 **rue** a bitter herb

ACT IV

SCENE 1   Richard yields his crown to Henry

This scene occupies the whole of Act IV, and is made up of four distinct incidents.

1 **Lines 1–106.** The scene opens with Henry asking Bagot for details of the circumstances of Gloucester's death. His enquiries lead to a series of challenges and counter-challenges as the noblemen present argue fiercely about whether Aumerle was or was not responsible for Gloucester's murder.

This behaviour recalls, and contrasts with, the opening of the play, when Richard sat in judgement on a quarrel about Gloucester's death. That had been a formal and splendid occasion. As Henry is about to begin his reign, he too sits in judgement on a similar quarrel, but this is an unruly, almost ridiculous, squabble. Who actually accuses whom of what is less important than the impression of violent disorder which is created, and which is built up to almost comic proportions (Aumerle, for example, runs out of gages with which to challenge people). It appears that Henry's reign – his 'new world' (line 78) – is going to be less grand, less splendid, than Richard's. Thus Shakespeare begins the scene by impressing on the audience that, whatever Richard's failings, something fine is lost when he ceases to be king.

2 **Lines 107–61.** York enters to announce that Richard will willingly give up the crown, and he hails Henry Bolingbroke as King Henry IV. At this the Bishop of Carlisle protests and, in a speech crucial to the political ideas of the play, he argues that no subject can possibly judge, let alone depose, a true sovereign, and that if the noblemen present recognise Henry as King, then the rivalries among the descendants of Edward III for the throne will result in civil war for years to come. For this intervention, the Bishop is arrested on a charge of treason, and entrusted to the Abbot of Westminster's control.

Coming just prior to Richard's entry, the Bishop of Carlisle's speech serves to encourage the audience to sympathise with the deposed king rather than to support his usurping successor. The Bishop rehearses the arguments on Richard's side, stresses the enormity of what is about to happen, and warns of its terrible and lasting consequences in words which the Elizabethan audience would know were fulfilled in the fifteenth-century Wars of the Roses. Shakespeare is thus arranging the scene to win a sympathetic hearing for Richard. The Bishop's arrest, however, is a stark demonstration that political power will prevail whatever the arguments: nothing will prevent Henry carrying through his plan.

3 **Lines 162–319.** The deposition scene follows. To justify his action, Henry has planned that Richard should publicly announce his willingness to give up the throne and read out a list of those crimes he has committed which make him unfit to rule. Richard does abdicate, but cannot bring himself to read out the list. Eventually, Henry tells Northumberland not to compel him to do so.

Although it is Henry who has arranged the affair, he says very little; it is Richard who is the centre of attention. He is in a confused state of mind, worn out by sadness, oppressed by the hopelessness of his situation and (as he believes) the injustice of what is happening. The spectacle of a man thus reduced to nothing is deeply moving and serves again to win sympathy from Henry to Richard.

4 **Lines 320–33.** Finally we hear, in the conversation between the Abbot of Westminster, the Bishop of Carlisle and Aumerle, of a plot to overthrow Henry and to restore Richard.

No sooner is Henry on the throne than troubles follow. Here is immediate fulfilment of the Bishop of Carlisle's prophecy: once power has been taken from its legitimate holder, civil disorder ensues. Thus, in the very scene in which Henry achieves kingship it is evident that his authority will not be easily or generally accepted and that his will not be a quiet reign. Once again, the audience is prevented from straightforwardly approving of Henry's action.

In order to end on this note, and to encourage the audience to view Richard's predicament sympathetically throughout the scene, Shakespeare has both altered and speeded up the historical sequence of events. In Holinshed (see Shakespeare's Use of Sources), the order is as follows (the paragraph numbers of the above summaries are used to indicate Shakespeare's rearrangement of the material):

(3)	29 September 1399:	Richard abdicates
(2)	30 September 1399:	Henry takes the throne
(1)	16 October 1399:	Bagot accuses Aumerle
(2)	22 October 1399:	Carlisle's defence of Richard
(1)	27 October 1399:	Henry decides to send for Mowbray
(4)	December 1399:	The Abbot plots to restore Richard

s.d. **Fitzwater** Walter, Baron Fitzwalter (1368–?1406), a supporter of Henry

Surrey Sir Thomas Holland (1374–1400), Duke of Surrey and Earl of Kent, finally executed for his staunch opposition to Henry (see V.6.8, where he is referred to as 'Kent'). It seems that Shakespeare did not identify him with the Lord Marshal in I.1 and I.3 (see pages 15 and 26 of this Note)

1 **Bagot** it seems that Shakespeare assumes Bagot has deserted Richard's cause and is now co-operating with Henry, although he had planned to (and historically did) go to Ireland (II.2.140)

4 **Who wrought it with** either 'who persuaded' or 'who collaborated with'

5 **timeless** untimely

10–19 **In that … death** the chronology is incorrect here: Gloucester was killed in 1397, long before Henry was banished in the autumn of 1398, so Aumerle

could not have remarked at the time of Gloucester's death (lines 10, 14)
that he would rather Henry never returned from banishment (lines 15–17)

13 **Calais** the port in northern France where Gloucester was murdered
uncle Gloucester

21 **fair stars** noble rank (since this was supposedly due to the favourable
influence of the stars at his birth)

22 **equal terms** a knight was not bound to fight with his social inferior, and
compared to Aumerle (grandson of Edward III), Bagot is 'base' (line 20)

25 **manual seal of death** a legal document receives its authority from the seal
placed on it to prove it is valid; Aumerle's gesture with his hand ('manual')
is the proof (or 'seal') that he will kill his accuser

29 **temper** quality and, more specifically, brightness of the blade of a sword

31–2 **Excepting ... so** I wish that the man who has so angered ('moved') me was
the best knight in this company ('presence') with the exception of one
(namely, Henry)

33 **sympathy** equal rank

40 **rapier** light, narrow sword with a point used for thrusting; it was coming
into fashion in England in Shakespeare's time but was quite unknown in the
fourteenth century

52 **I task the earth to the like** I lay on the earth a similar task (namely, to
support my gage)

54 **hollowed** shouted, hollered

55 **sun to sun** sunrise to sunset (the prescribed limits for a combat)

56 **Engage it to the trial** accept the challenge

65 **boy** a term of contempt here

66 **That lie** namely, Fitzwater's charge (line 65) that Surrey lied when he said
(line 64) that it was a lie that Aumerle boasted of killing Gloucester (lines
35–7)

72 **fondly** needlessly
forward willing (that is, line 71 is needless as Fitzwater is only too ready to
accept)

76 **There is my bond of faith** this refers to Fitzwater's gage (either another
thrown down, or the one thrown down to challenge Aumerle at line 34)

78 **new world** the new order of things established by Henry

80 **Norfolk** Mowbray (see page 15 of this Note)

83 **Some honest Christian trust me with a gage** Aumerle has already used one on
Bagot (line 24) and one at lines 56–7

86 **rest under gage** remain as challenges (and not come to trial yet)

94 **Streaming the ensign of the Christian cross** a red cross was the badge of the Crusaders (see line 100), which Carlisle imagines blowing ('Streaming') on a flag ('ensign') as Mowbray charges the enemy

95 **pagans** in fact Muslims

Saracens Arabs

103–4 **the bosom / Of good old Abraham** heaven (Luke 16:22)

108 **plume-plucked** humbled

115–16 **Worst ... truth** though, as a bishop, I may be the least important person ('Worst' meaning 'lowest rank' here) to speak in this royal company, yet it best becomes me (rather than anyone else) to speak the truth

123 **but** except when

by present

130 **refined** purified (by their Christian faith)

141 **kind** fellow countrymen

142 **mutiny** discord, strife

144 **Golgotha** the Hebrew name for the hill where Christ was crucified (Matthew 27:33), translated as 'a place of a skull' in the King James Bible (1611), but as 'a place of dead men's skulls' in the earlier Bible translation available at the time of the play's composition (the Geneva Bible, 1560)

145 **this house against this house** the family (or 'house') of Plantagenet, which was indeed to divide into the rival houses of York (descendants of the Duke of York) and Lancaster (descendants of Gaunt)

149 **child, child's children** three generations hence

154 **commons' suit** the request of the House of Commons (which had asked that the reasons for Richard's loss of his throne should be publicly stated)

157 **conduct** conductor

159 **Procure your sureties** produce your guarantees that you will appear on the day appointed (the surety would probably take the form of a lord willing to swear that he would ensure the appellant comes)

161 **looked for** expected (the way you have behaved)

173 **clerk** the assistant at a Christian service who would make the response 'Amen' to the priest's prayers

184 **owes** owns, is equipped with

194–8 **Your cares ... they stay** the sense of 'care' changes throughout this teasing passage, which can be paraphrased as follows: Your taking on of responsibility ('Your cares') does not take away my troubles ('my cares').

My cause of grief ('My care') is that I have lost the responsibility of kingship ('loss of care') through the follies ('old care') I committed ('done'). Your source of worry ('Your care') is that you have gained responsibility ('gain of care') through the care with which you have carried out your recent plans ('by new care won'). Although I have given you the worries of office ('The cares I give') I have troubles still ('I have'), though apparently given to you, since I cannot give away the crown without guilt, regret and shame. Anxiety and sorrow may attend the crown ("tend the crown'), yet they remain with me though I am no longer the king

200 **Ay, no. No, ay; for I must nothing be** 'Ay' (yes) and 'I' sound alike; the puns suggest both Richard's indecision ('yes, no, no, yes') and his despair ('I am nothing, no "I" exists'), as well as the torment of a mind now powerless to do anything but play with words

201 **Therefore no no, for I resign to thee** as you can see, I am not contented, but I do resign in your favour

202 **undo** both 'undress' (as Richard removes the symbols of kingship) and 'ruin'

215 **with nothing grieved** both 'grieved with having nothing' and 'grieved by nothing'

224 **profit** prosperity

228 **weaved-up** continues the **image** of 'ravel out' (literally, to pull out a thread from a piece of cloth or ball of thread): Richard will have to state each single detail (or thread) of all the foolish actions (the cloth) of his life

238 **Pilate** Pontius Pilate, unable to discover clear proof of guilt in Jesus, washed his hands when he condemned Jesus, to show he was not responsible for Jesus's death (Matthew 27:24)

240 **sour cross** bitter suffering (Jesus was put to death on a cross)

245 **sort** gang (a contemptuous word)

249 **pompous** surrounded with pomp, splendid

251 **state** grandeur, royal rank

263 **sterling** valid

284 **faced** allowed, countenanced

291 **The shadow of your sorrow** the consequence of your sorrow (that is, breaking the glass); in line 292 'shadow' refers simply to the image

294 **'Tis very true** Henry's dismissive lines (lines 291–2) had tried to stop Richard's performance by pointing out that he had broken only a mirror and that he had not, as claimed (line 290), been destroyed by sorrow; Richard takes up the word 'shadow' to agree with Henry, but in the following lines, argues that his actions are the consequences (or shadows) of a *real* grief, just as the mirror reflected (shadowed) a real face

296 **to** of

307 **to** to be

314 **from your sights** out of the sight of all of you

316 **Conveyors** a pun on 'convey' in the sense of 'steal'

327-8 **take the Sacrament / To bury mine intents** swear on the Sacrament (the consecrated bread of the Holy Communion service) to conceal my plans

ACT V

SCENE 1   In London the Queen and Richard are parted as he is sent to confinement in Pomfret Castle

The Queen, who has come to London to seek out Richard (III.4.96–7), meets him on his way to the Tower, where he was despatched by Henry (IV.1.315). She is dismayed at the change in him and, especially, at his loss of will to fight back at his enemies. Northumberland interrupts them to say that Richard is now to go to Pomfret in Yorkshire, and not the Tower, and that the Queen must leave for France. Richard foretells that Northumberland and Henry will fall out before long, but Northumberland is not impressed and hurries to part the two. They take their last farewell in great sadness.

This is the last of the three scenes by which Shakespeare wins sympathy for Richard through Queen Isabel (see also II.2 and III.4). The political **tragedy** of Richard, depicted in IV.1, is followed now by the personal tragedy. In Richard's own words, he is 'Doubly divorced', the violation of his marriage now following the violation of his marriage to his country (lines 71–3).

2 **Julius Caesar's ill-erected Tower** the Tower of London, wrongly supposed to have been first built by Julius Caesar

3 **flint** flinty, made of stone; thus (**metaphorically**) cold, unfeeling

7 **soft** wait

11 **model where old Troy did stand** emblem of fallen greatness, like the great city of Troy after it had been sacked by the Greeks. Tradition had it that London was founded by refugees from Troy who named it 'New Troy'

12 **map** form, image
King Richard's tomb because Richard's kingship has died, this man has only the body or form of the King

13–15 **Thou ... guest?** Richard is the 'beauteous inn' filled with grief, Henry the 'alehouse' where triumph is entertained

24 **new world's crown** a crown of righteousness in heaven

25 **Which our profane hours here have thrown down** either 'since our wicked lives here have lost us our earthly crown' or 'which crown of righteousness our wicked lives here have thrown away'

31 **To be** because he is

35 **If aught but beasts** if of anything other than beasts (implying that only because Richard's noblemen have behaved like animals is he no longer a king of men)

37 **sometimes** former

43 **quite** requite, answer
griefs tragic tales

46 **For why** because (of the tale's sadness)

52 **Pomfret** Pontefract, in Yorkshire

55–9 **Northumberland, thou ladder ... corruption** in *Henry IV Part 2*, III.1.60–79, Henry quotes these lines when their prophecy has been fulfilled

67 **one or both** the King or the man who helped him to the throne, or both

75 **kiss** bride and groom complete the marriage ceremony with a kiss

77 **pines the clime** consumes or wears away the land

80 **Hallowmas** All Saints' Day, now 1 November, but in Shakespeare's time 12 November and so near the shortest day of the year, 22 December

84 **That were some love, but little policy** the **quartos** (see Note on the Text) give this line to Richard, the first **folio** to Northumberland, whose down-to-earth shrewdness it seems to suit better; 'little policy' means 'bad politics'

88 **Better far off than, near, be ne'er the nea'er** it is better to be far apart than, being close together, to be no nearer seeing each other

90 **So longest way shall have the longest moans** as the Queen is going all the way to France she will have the most moaning to do if line 89 is carried out literally

92 **piece** lengthen

98 **To take on me to keep and kill thy heart** to undertake to look after your heart and then kill it (when I die of grief)

101 **We make woe wanton** we play with grief

SCENE 2   **York discovers that his son, Aumerle, is involved in the conspiracy against Henry, and, despite the pleas of the Duchess, determines to tell the King**

When the scene opens, the Duke of York is telling his wife of the humiliating way in which Henry brought Richard to London (which had happened between III.3 and IV.1). When York's son, Aumerle, enters, York insists on reading a paper he sees his son is carrying, and from it he learns that Aumerle is involved in the Abbot of Westminster's plot to restore Richard to the throne. As York has taken an oath of allegiance to Henry, and has personally guaranteed the loyalty of his son, he is furious at this discovery and determines, despite his wife's pleas, to ride immediately to reveal the plot to the King. The Duchess sends Aumerle to reach Henry before York, and herself sets out immediately to follow.

The Abbot's plot was actually discovered in January 1400, but from York's recounting in this scene of Richard's arrival in London, it appears to come to light immediately after that happened, in September 1399. This telescoping of events creates the impression that Henry's reign begins in discord and that the new regime has not a single moment of unchallenged authority (see also Act IV).

The account of Richard and Henry's entry into London serves, yet again, to win sympathy for Richard as York tells of his dignified bearing under the crowd's insults.

s.d. **Duchess** actually York's second wife (Aumerle's mother, Isabella of Castile, died in 1394), but Shakespeare makes the Duchess behave and speak (see line 103) as though she is Aumerle's mother, not his step-mother

9 **seemed to know** the 'steed' is the subject of the verb here, i.e. the horse seemed to understand his ambitious rider

15 **and that** and you would have thought that

16 **painted imagery** the walls of Elizabethan houses were often hung with tapestries and painted cloths depicting people with words coming out of their mouths

38 **we bound our calm contents** we must submit ourselves to calm content

41–3 **Aumerle ... Rutland now** York's son was deprived of the dukedom of Aumerle for his part in the quarrel depicted at the beginning of IV.1 and should now be known by his other title, Earl of Rutland

45 **fealty** faithfulness

46–7 **Who ... spring?** who are the new favourites at court?

52 **justs and triumphs** jousts or tournaments, and processions

56 **seal** the red wax sign, by which a letter was signed and sealed, might hang down from it on a narrow strip of parchment; it could therefore be outside Aumerle's clothes while the letter itself is in an inner pocket

67–8 **Bound to himself ... fool** York rounds on his wife since, if her suggestion is correct, and Aumerle has a bond to borrow money, the document promising repayment would be with the creditor who lent the money

79 **appeach** accuse

85 **Poor boy, thou art amazed** the Duchess supposes that Aumerle is stunned by what is happening, as he does not strike the servant

86 **villain** man (used to a servant without suggestion of criminality)

89 **own** own family

90 **Have we more sons?** historically, York did have another son, Richard, Earl of Cambridge, who appears in *Henry V*

91 **teeming-date** years of child-bearing

97–9 **A dozen ... Oxford** as the Abbot of Westminster had planned, IV.1.325–9; 'interchangeably set down their hands' means that each conspirator has a document signed by all, so each has a record of the others' oaths

100 **Then what is that to him?** then what have their actions got to do with him?

SCENE 3 **The plot is revealed to Henry, who pardons Aumerle but condemns the other conspirators**

The first twenty-two lines of the scene show Henry concerned about the dissolute and irresponsible behaviour of his son, who frequents taverns and mocks the ideals of noble society. Aumerle then enters, and the action follows directly on from V.2. In private audience with the King he begs Henry's pardon, which is granted before Henry can learn what it is that Aumerle planned to do. York is then admitted and he reveals the plot. He argues strongly that Aumerle should not be pardoned, but then the Duchess arrives and she argues, just as strongly, that he should be. Henry finally confirms the pardon he has granted, but arranges for the other conspirators to be captured and put to death.

A situation verging on the comic arose at the beginning of IV.1 with the repeated challenges of the nobles. This lessened respect for the new King's reign and was a marked contrast to the deposition which followed. After the sombre mood of V.1, relief came again in the near-comedy of York struggling to put on his boots in V.2 while the Duchess tried to prevent him. The same mood prevails here, with the succession of people banging on the door and the husband and wife contradicting each other so vehemently. Henry himself recognises that this is approaching **farce** (lines 78–9). A comparison with Richard is all in Richard's favour: this scene deprives Henry of all pretension to regality, even as that quality is about to be finally extinguished with Richard's death.

The son to whom Henry refers at the opening of the scene does not appear in this play, but, as Prince Hal, he will have a leading role in the *Henry IV* plays and, as Henry V, he will personify the ideal king in *Henry V*. Henry's speech introduces what is to be the main theme of *Henry IV Part 1*: Hal's apparent unsuitability to inherit the throne. The speech may thus indicate that Shakespeare already had that play in mind when he composed *Richard II* (see p. 69), but here its purpose is to add to the quarrelling nobles of IV.1, and to the conspiracy about which Henry is to learn in a moment, another anxiety for this troubled king: the character of his heir. It seems that to gain the throne is the least of the challenges Henry must face: securing it and bequeathing it are far more difficult. Henry is indeed beset with those 'cares' described by Richard in IV.1.194–8.

9 **watch** night watchmen

passengers travellers

10 **effeminate** self-indulgent (see Critical History on Feminist Approaches)

11 **Takes on the point** takes it to be a point

15 **gallant** fine young man (used sarcastically here)

16 **stews** brothels

17 **commonest creature** meanest prostitute

19 **lustiest** most vigorous

31 **Unless a** unless I receive a

34 **after-love** future loyalty

42 **secure foolhardy** over-confident and rash

43 **Shall I for love speak treason to thy face?** must I, because of my love and loyalty, speak treason (by calling you foolhardy) to your face?

49 **my haste forbids me show** my haste prevents me from explaining (because I am so short of breath)

60 **sheer** pure

65 **digressing** wayward

66 **bawd** literally, a woman who procures prostitutes for men; thus an encourager to vice

79 **'The Beggar and the King'** a reference to the ballad of King Cophetua who fell in love with a beggar-maid: Henry means that the situation is becoming absurd, like the subject of the ballad

84-5 **This festered ... confound** if you cut off this poisoned limb (Aumerle), the rest of the body (the court) will remain healthy, but if you leave it alone it will infect and destroy all the rest

87 **itself** its own flesh and blood, its child

none other can one cannot love another (and so not you, the King)

89 **dugs** breasts

rear raise (by getting Aumerle pardoned and so raised to life)

91-5 **Not ... boy** the Duchess pleads with Henry as she vowed to do in V.2.117-8

101 **breast** heart

116 **but not so short as sweet** but it is sweeter than it is short

118 **'Pardonne-moi'** French: a polite way of refusing a request ('pardon me, but ...')

119 **Dost thou teach pardon pardon to destroy?** a reference to York's use of the word in the previous line: he teaches the King how to refuse to give a pardon by actually using the word 'pardon'

122 **current** valid (i.e. with its English meaning)

123 **chopping French** French, which changes the meaning of words

124 **Set thy tongue there** let your tongue express (the pity I see in your eye)

125 **Or in thy piteous heart plant thou thine ear** the Duchess's point is that by doing this Henry would hear how his heart responds to their plea

133 **twain** weaken by splitting in two

136 **brother-in-law** John Holland, Duke of Exeter (?1352–1400), who married Henry's sister Elizabeth. He lost his dukedom at the same time as Aumerle and is mentioned at II.1.281, but has no part in the play

the Abbot the Abbot of Westminster, who began the plot (see IV.1.320–33)

145 **I pray God make thee new** a proverbial saying, deriving from the claim in 2 Corinthians 5:17 that any man in Christ is a 'new creature'; it means, in effect, 'let's make a new start' scene 4   **Sir Piers of Exton resolves to murder Richard**

Sir Piers of Exton, a courtier who has overheard Henry say he wished Richard were no longer alive to pose a threat to him, resolves to perform what he takes to be the will of the King: the murder of Richard.

This short scene is based upon Holinshed's explanation of how Richard's death came about (see also Shakespeare's Use of Sources). Richard would be a source of anxiety to Henry because, as long as he lived, former supporters might still be loyal to him and seek to restore him to the throne despite his supposedly willing abdication. For this reason, Richard's death might be expected to secure Henry's kingship.

The scene advances the plot, but its main dramatic function is to ensure that foreboding and suspense play over the next scene since the audience will now watch V.5 in the knowledge that Richard's murder is imminent.

s.d. **Sir Piers of Exton** nothing is known about this nobleman, except that he was said to have murdered Richard

Man servant

7 **wishtly** longingly, intently

9 **divorce** separate, take away

11 **rid** rid him of

scene 5   **Richard is murdered in Pomfret Castle**

Alone in prison in Pomfret Castle, Richard meditates upon his situation. He analyses his condition by comparing his thoughts and prison to people and the world, his life to incorrectly played music, and his prolonged sadness to the hours of a clock. A groom enters and expresses his sorrow at Richard's plight, followed by a gaoler who refuses to follow his usual custom of tasting Richard's food. At this, Richard realises his last moment is come. He puts up a brave resistance, but is overcome by Exton and his companions. The scene ends with Exton regretting the murder as soon as it has been committed.

This scene completes the process, begun in II.2 immediately after Richard left for Ireland, whereby our sympathy tends towards

Richard. The body of the scene is devoted to one of Shakespeare's most moving **soliloquies**. Its effect of **pathos** is reinforced by the affection and loyalty shown for the doomed Richard by the groom, one of those common people for whom his reign has supposedly been so disastrous. To sympathy is added admiration as Richard stoutly resists the murderers: 'As full of valour as of royal blood' says Exton (line 113). Shakespeare thus contrives for Richard a scene in which a hero is **tragically** killed rather than a tyrant justly assassinated.

The murder occurred on 14 February 1400.

8 **still-breeding thoughts** thoughts which themselves multiply

9 **this little world** his prison (see line 21)

10 **humours** various temperaments, types
this world the real world outside the prison

13-14 **set the word itself / Against the word** Richard means that when a man thinks of God (line 12), he finds himself confused by apparent contradictions in the Bible (the Word of God)

14-17 **'Come ... eye.'** the original versions of these two texts come close together in the gospels of Matthew (19:14, 24), Mark (10:14, 25) and Luke (18:16, 25): they are apparently contradictory in that the first seems to invite all to follow Christ while the second implies that it is extremely difficult, if not impossible, to do so. Biblical scholars then and now have disputed the meaning of the second text: the sense may be either that it is difficult for a camel to pass through a small gate in a city wall ('needle'), or for a rope (made from camel's hair) to pass through a needle's eye: in Richard's words 'postern' (small door) suggests the former, but 'thread' the latter, so it seems that Shakespeare was well aware of the difficulty and chose his words deliberately to heighten the ambiguity and thereby give weight to Richard's point (lines 12–13) that 'thoughts of things divine' are troubled by 'scruples' (doubts)

18 **Thoughts tending to ambition** Richard continues to illustrate his point by turning, after divine thoughts (line 12), to worldly thoughts of ambition

19 **nails** fingernails

22 **And for they cannot** and because they cannot (that is, ambitious thoughts cannot achieve this wonder, lines 18–19)

25 **seely** simple-minded

26 **refuge their shame** seek refuge from their shame

31 **Thus play I in one person many people** by entertaining these different kinds of thoughts (lines 11, 18, 23), which are the people of his world (lines 6–10), Richard now goes on to show how, in his mind, he can assume different roles

41 **being nothing** dead (the conclusion to the thought Richard introduced at line 11, that we are never content in our minds)

43 **time** rhythm

no proportion kept the melody and notes are not properly played

44 **the music of men's lives** Richard now compares a well-ordered life to a well-played piece of music

46 **check** rebuke

string stringed instrument

47 **my** my own (emphatic: Richard can hear when another plays badly but did not notice when he ruled badly)

state kingdom

time life

48 **time** rhythm (the 'music' of his life)

50 **numbering clock** clock which tells the hours

51–4 **My thoughts are minutes ... tears** here Richard moves on to a third **image** (after 'world' and 'music'). In these complex lines Richard expresses the hopelessness and futility of his position by seeing himself as having nothing to do but mark the passing of time with his grief. The sense might be paraphrased as follows: Since I now have nothing to do but watch time pass, my thoughts are like minutes, only ways of measuring time. And, as my thoughts are sad ones, so the sighs they cause mark out the passage of time ('Their watches') like the ticks ('jars') made by the pendulum of a clock. But instead of looking at a clock dial to tell the time, time for me is registered in the tears in my eyes ('unto mine eyes'), which thus become themselves like the outer edge of a clock face ('outward watch') to which my finger points, like a clock hand ('dial's point') as it wipes away my tears

58 **my time** the time which should have been Richard II's

60 **jack** a figure of a man which on some clocks strikes the hours and quarters

62 **holp** helped (music was thought to cure madness)

66 **strange brooch** rare jewel

67–8 **royal ... noble ... groats** puns on coins: a royal was worth ten shillings (or 120 pence), a noble six shillings and eight pence (or eighty pence) and a groat four pence. The difference between a royal and a noble was thus forty pence, or ten groats; so Richard means that in calling him 'royal' the groom has valued him too highly, as he is now merely the groom's equal ('peer')

76 **earned** grieved

78 **Barbary** a breed of horse, but also here the name of Richard's own horse

86 **clapping** patting

94 **jaucing** the movement of a rider in the saddle

99 **Taste of it first, as thou art wont to do** Richard wants to be sure it is not poisoned

105 **What means death in this rude assault?** either 'do you mean to kill me with this vicious attack?' or 'what does death mean by coming on me so suddenly in this vicious attack?'

SCENE 6   **Henry receives news of Richard's death and, refusing the murderer reward, proposes a crusade to expiate his guilt**

Henry receives news that the rebels have been defeated and executed, with the exception of the Bishop of Carlisle, whom Henry allows to live in a monastery. Exton then brings in the body of Richard. Henry, though he admits Richard's death is convenient for him, is appalled at the murder and refuses Exton thanks or reward and proposes a crusade to make amends for what has been done in his name.

The play ends not in triumph and rejoicing, even though Henry now has the crown, the rebels are defeated and Richard is dead, but in sadness and guilt: Henry is 'full of woe / That blood should sprinkle me to make me grow' (lines 45–6). It is now March 1400, not quite two years since Henry charged Mowbray with treason.

2 **rebels** the 'dozen' mentioned by York in V.2.97 who, when the plot to kill Henry was discovered (V.2–3), rose in open rebellion

3 **Ciceter** Cirencester

8 **The heads** the heads of traitors were stuck on poles on London Bridge **Salisbury, Spencer, Blunt, and Kent** for Salisbury see the beginning of II.4; Spencer is Thomas Le Despenser (1373–1400), Earl of Gloucester, who lost his earldom at the same time as Aumerle (see V.2.41–3); Blunt is Sir Thomas Blount; for Kent see the note on Surrey at the beginning of IV.1

s.d. **Fitzwater** see the beginning of IV.1

14 **Brocas and Sir Bennet Seely** Sir Leonard Brokas and Sir Bennet Seely were supporters of Richard

20 **clog** burden

23 **of his pride** for what his pride led him to do

25 **reverent room** religious retreat (monastery)

26 **More than thou hast** a situation more withdrawn and religious than you have occupied in the past

34–6 **for thou ... land** what you have done with your deadly hand has brought disgrace and shame on me and this famous land

43 **Cain** after he murdered his brother Abel, Cain was condemned to wander the earth as an outcast (Genesis 4:10–16)

48 **incontinent** immediately

49 **make a voyage to the Holy Land** undertake a crusade to Jerusalem as a form of penance

PART THREE

CRITICAL APPROACHES

RICHARD II & SHAKESPEARE'S HISTORY PLAYS

William Shakespeare wrote ten history plays in all. Of these, one – *Henry VIII* – was written at the end of his career (1612–13), long after the other history plays, and one – *King John* (1597) – dealt with an isolated period of early medieval English history to which Shakespeare did not return. The remaining eight plays, however, belong together. They dramatise the course of English history from the fall of Richard II in 1399 to the death of Richard III in 1485. These eight plays thus form a sequence which covers nearly a century of English history, but they were not written in the order of the events which that sequence depicts. Rather, they were composed in two groups, of four plays each, the earlier group dealing with the later period of history. The two groups (or tetralogies) are:

- First Tetralogy – written between 1590 and 1593, this consists of the three parts of *Henry VI*, and *Richard III*, covering 1422–85
- Second Tetralogy – written between 1595 and 1598/9, this consists of *Richard II*, the two parts of *Henry IV*, and *Henry V*, covering 1399–1422

Richard II was first published in 1597, and scholars now believe it was written and first performed in 1595. Thus, when Shakespeare turned to *Richard II* in 1595 he had completed the first tetralogy; that is to say, he had written the end of the story and was now turning to its beginning. And he followed *Richard II* with the two parts of *Henry IV* and *Henry V* in order. This suggests that when he began *Richard II* he may have already formulated the idea of a complete cycle of plays and that he wrote the play not only as a drama in its own right, but as a prologue to the full cycle of plays which he then went on to complete. This view may draw support from the many prophecies in *Richard II* of the suffering and bloodshed that England will endure because of Richard's failings as king and his deposition by Henry (e.g. II.1.200–8, II.2.9–12, III.3.93–100, IV.1.134–49, V.1.55–68; see also Tragic Loss, pp. 80–2 of this Note). That so many people foretell civil war stresses the fact that the events depicted in *Richard II* will have dire consequences in the future that lies beyond the play – that is, in the years which are treated in Shakespeare's other history plays. This is underlined by the end of the play, which does not have any satisfying neatness, any sense of completion or **closure**, about it. Henry has already suffered the Abbot of Westminster's rebellion, he is worried about his son's fitness to inherit the throne, and he feels guilt and remorse for Richard's death. There is no sense of triumph, of something finally achieved, in Henry's final speech. Clearly, though the action of *Richard II* ends Richard's story, it is only the beginning of a larger story.

THE ELIZABETHAN VIEW OF RICHARD II

It was no accident that it was the fifteenth century which Shakespeare chose to dramatise: this was a century which fascinated the Elizabethans, for whom it was of crucial significance. Their attention was held particularly by the reign of Richard and by his deposition, for to this they owed, ultimately, the presence on the throne of their own queen, Elizabeth I. In the minds of the Elizabethans the deposition of Richard II began a series of events which led to the Tudor dynasty and culminated in the reign of Elizabeth I.

This construction of fifteenth-century events is evident in the title of the prose chronicle history published in 1548 by Edward Hall, one of the sources for Shakespeare's play (see also Shakespeare's Use of Sources). Its full title was:

> *The Union of the Two Noble and Illustrious Families of Lancaster and York, being long in continual dissension for the crown of this noble realm, with all the acts done in both the times of the Princes, both of the one lineage and of the other, beginning at the time of king Henry the fourth, the first author of this division, and so successively proceeding to the reign of the high and prudent prince king Henry the eighth, the indubitable flower and very heir of both the said lineages.*

This title gives to the events of the preceding century a clear shape, and furthermore, a shape which is both meaningful and coherent, almost purposeful. In three ways, it imposes a structure upon the historical material which is the chronicle's subject:

- Fifteenth-century English history, from the accession of Henry IV in 1399 to the defeat and death of Richard III at the battle of Bosworth

Field in 1485, is presented as *a self-contained period with a single narrative thread*: 'dissension for the crown', the progress of the civil war, is the single focus and interest.

- This narrative has *a clear beginning* in the deposition of Richard II by Henry Bolingbroke. Richard was the last English king to rule by clear hereditary right, descended in direct succession from William the Conqueror (who ruled from 1066 to 1087), and to Edward Hall, as to the Elizabethans generally, the deposition of this rightful monarch was disastrous. Once the crown had been seized by a usurper, possession of it depended not upon right but upon might and it became the object of rivalry amongst powerful magnates and noblemen. The result was the series of military conflicts known as the Wars of the Roses, named from the badges of the contending factions: the House of Lancaster (the descendants of John of Gaunt, fourth son of Edward III, Duke of Lancaster, whose badge was a red rose) and the House of York (the descendants of Edmund of Langley, fifth son of Edward III, Duke of York, whose badge was a white rose).

- The narrative also has *a clear ending*. Henry Tudor defeated the last Yorkist king, Richard III, thereby becoming Henry VII. He claimed descent from John of Gaunt, Duke of Lancaster, and so, when he married the Yorkist heiress, Richard III's niece Elizabeth, the two warring families were at last united. Their son, Henry VIII, hence had no rival; his daughter was Elizabeth I.

Thus, for Edward Hall, and (in large part because of Hall) for Shakespeare and his fellow Elizabethans, the deposition of Richard II was the beginning of the historical story which ended with their own queen. Although at the time Shakespeare's play was written that event had occurred almost exactly two hundred years ago, it was very far from irrelevant to his audience or shut safely away in the past. It was both the original cause of the stable and ordered society in which they themselves lived, and a case study of how that stability might be lost through monarchical incompetence. The appeal to this precedent at the time of the rebellion of the Earl of Essex, and the sensitivity of Elizabeth to parallels between her reign and that of Richard II, is sufficient demonstration of its disturbing contemporary pertinence for the Elizabethans (see Note on the Text for further details).

Shakespeare did not invent his plots. Nearly every one of Shakespeare's plays has at least one known source. As this implies, the Renaissance notion of creativity did not identify it with originality (an idea which the modern age has inherited from the Romantics). Renaissance aesthetics identified it instead with the ingenious reworking of received stories and myths. Hence, Renaissance artists invariably took up subjects which their predecessors or contemporaries had already handled, in an attempt to surpass their presentation of these topics. Consequently, modern ideas of the integrity of the text and of an author's copyright in what he or she publishes were unknown. Any published text became public property, available to be reworked by anyone, or (as we might say today) to be misrepresented or plagiarised.

These very different ideas of artistic purpose and responsibility explain why, though Shakespeare based *Richard II*, as he did his other history plays, on the historical sources available to him, he felt no obligation to reproduce their account of events accurately. On the contrary, he took from his sources only those facts which would serve his requirements, and was quite ready to omit details or to change the order of events. It is clear that dramatic effectiveness, not historical accuracy, was his criterion.

The chief sources which scholars have identified for *Richard II* are:

1 Edward Hall, *The Union of the Two Noble and Illustrious Families of Lancaster and York* (1548): this chronicle history deals with the history of England from the end of Richard II's reign, through the Wars of the Roses, to Henry VII and the founding of the Tudor dynasty. It seems to have supplied the material for Act V Scenes 2–3, and may have suggested to Shakespeare the plan for his complete cycle of history plays (see also *Richard II* and Shakespeare's History Plays and The Elizabethan View of Richard II).

2 Raphael Holinshed, *Chronicles of England, Scotland and Ireland* (1586–7): Holinshed's account of Richard II's reign supplied the general outline of events and historical facts for Shakespeare's play.

3 Jean Froissart, *Chroniques*, translated into English by John Bourchier, Lord Berners (1523–5): Froissart was a Frenchman who visited Edward III's court in the 1360s and actually lived at Richard II's court. His account is very sympathetic to Richard, and may have suggested to

Shakespeare the noble character of Gaunt (who in Holinshed is an ignoble self-seeker) and the idea for Gaunt's last speeches and rebukes to Richard in Act II Scene 1.

4 Samuel Daniel, *The Civil Wars between Lancaster and York* (1595): this long poem probably supplied the clue for the love between Richard and his queen (Daniel, like Shakespeare, makes her older than she actually was) and may have suggested the scene of their parting, Act V Scene 1.

5 *Thomas of Woodstock* (not published until 1870): this anonymous play, about the Duke of Gloucester and his murder, deals with Richard II's reign between 1382 and 1397 – that is, with the events immediately preceding those in Shakespeare's play. It may have suggested the favourable view of Gloucester we find in *Richard II* – 'plain well-meaning soul' (II.1.128) – and the character of the Duchess of Gloucester (Act I Scene 2). Perhaps Shakespeare took the idea of presenting Gaunt as a wise and patriotic counsellor from the similar presentation of Gloucester in *Woodstock*. However, although it is agreed that this play dates from the Elizabethan period, it is extant in only a single manuscript and was not printed until the nineteenth century; so there can be no certainty that it was actually written or available to Shakespeare before he composed *Richard II*.

6 George Ferrers, William Baldwin and others, *The Mirror for Magistrates* (1559): this massive collection of verse tales about the **tragic** fall of princes and nobles includes the stories of the Duke of Gloucester, Thomas Mowbray, the Earl of Northumberland and Richard II himself, and may have given Shakespeare hints for a number of details.

Shakespeare's handling of these sources, and his different ways of moulding his material, may be summarised as follows:

- The omission of unsuitable material. Richard's campaign in Ireland, of which we hear nothing (not even whether it was a success or not) is a notable example of this. By such omissions Shakespeare gives a clear and simple line to the action of the play, which is confined to Richard's decline and Henry's rise, without any digressions.
- The manipulation of events. A conspicuous example is that in Holinshed Northumberland takes Richard to Flint Castle as a prisoner, while in *Richard II* Henry and Northumberland find Richard there unexpectedly. This change makes Henry appear less cunning and less

active – more the favourite of fortune – than in Holinshed.

- The reordering of events. For a dramatically effective example of this, see Summaries & Commentaries, Act IV Scene 1.

- The telescoping of events. To gain momentum, to heighten dramatic tension, and to suggest a providential inevitability about the course of events, Shakespeare runs together incidents which were in fact separated in time (as, for example, in Act II Scene 1, where events covering six months appear to follow one another directly).

- The alteration of characters' ages and relationships. Examples include the depiction of the Queen (actually only eleven years old in 1399) as a mature woman, which enhances the **pathos** of her sorrow for Richard, and the presentation of the Duchess of York as Aumerle's natural mother (historically she was his step-mother), making her anxiety about his fate the more desperate (V.2.103–11).

- The addition of invented material. Examples of additions to the source material include Gaunt's famous speech in II.1.31–68, the behaviour of the Duchess of York in Act V Scenes 2–3, and – most significantly – the three scenes centred on the Queen (II.2.1–72, III.4, V.1). Only for the last of these was there a clue, in Daniel (for their purpose, see the Summaries & Commentaries).

- The introduction of recurrent **images** and **symbols**. Such **motifs** include the frequent sun imagery (see p. 90 of this Note), the crown (mentioned throughout the play, notably in III.2.160–77 and in IV.1.180–8, where it is used by Richard as a stage property), and references to mirrors and shadows (notably in IV.1.263–301), which, by **metaphorically** enriching the drama, serve both to heighten its dramatic moments and to articulate its recurrent themes.

- The isolation of the figure of Richard. Shakespeare centres his play more firmly than any source on the figure of Richard himself, devoting much attention (especially after the return from Ireland in Act III Scene 2) to the confusions and despair of Richard's mind and to the **pathos** and **tragedy** of his situation.

- The introduction of details in anticipation of the later *Henry IV* plays. The mention of Prince Hal (V.3.1–12) and the youth of Harry Percy (II.3.36–44) are examples of details which serve little purpose in *Richard II* but which clearly anticipate the situation Shakespeare was to handle in both parts of *Henry IV*.

In contrast to many Renaissance plays, in which multiple plots and the juxtaposition of different dramatic moods are common, *Richard II* is a remarkably uncluttered play. It has a very simple plot with a single focus of dramatic interest throughout. The main sequence of events drives steadily forward, and, except for the York family business in Act V Scenes 2–3, attention is never diverted from the interlocking fortunes of Richard and Henry by either digression or subordinate action. Although the play is divided up into five acts, this is an artificial structure imposed on the text after Shakespeare's death – none of the plays printed during his lifetime contained act or scene divisions (see also Background on Shakespeare's Theatre). In fact, the plot proceeds in four clear stages:

- Richard as king (I.1–II.1)
- The rise of Henry (II.2–III.1)
- The transference of power (III.2–IV.1)
- Henry as king (V.1–6)

As king, Richard banishes Henry; Henry returns; Richard yields to him; Henry is king. The pivotal scene, the turning point of this action, is Act III Scene 2, in which Richard, having returned from Ireland, abandons all hope of defeating Henry. He has effectively capitulated: from this moment there can be no doubt as to the outcome.

Simple though it is, there is something odd about the action of this play. In III.2 Richard has yet to confront the returned Henry, but, from his high hopes and optimism at the beginning of the scene, he comes to such deep despair by its end that he discharges his followers. Henry has won without a fight. There is no action, and certainly no confrontation, in the scene, but the crown has effectively passed from Richard to Henry. What follows, in the scenes in Act III which trace Henry's unopposed progress through England and in the deposition scene (IV.1), does not so much bring about the fall of Richard as enact what has already occurred. Rather than effect a change in the state of things, it is in some sense a public demonstration that the state of things has changed.

There are other examples in the play of events happening without any struggle. The opening of II.3 shows Henry crossing Gloucestershire with his army, but he seems to be engaged almost on a sight-seeing tour, or a triumphal progress, rather than an invasion. There is no opposition at all, and at the end of the scene, York, who has boasted that the power of the King lies in him (II.3.95–7), simply admits that he cannot stop the invader and invites Henry to spend the night at Berkeley Castle. Merely by arriving, Henry is transformed from York's foe to his guest. Similarly, in III.1, Henry has apparently captured Bushy and Green with the greatest of ease, and he simply has them executed.

What is remarkable, then, is that, most unusually for a history play, this is a play in which almost nothing physically happens. In I.3 we have all the ceremony and pomp of a trial but, just as the combat is about to begin, it is stopped. There is an army of Welshmen who, instead of fighting, simply fade away (II.4). There is a struggle between a monarch and a usurper, but it is a very peculiar kind of struggle. Henry foresees his meeting with Richard thus (III.3.54–7):

> Methinks King Richard and myself should meet
> With no less terror than the elements
> Of fire and water when their thundering shock
> At meeting tears the cloudy cheeks of heaven.

There is, however, no such great and elemental conflict as these lines suggest. Richard and Henry meet at Flint Castle with no 'shock' at all: they exchange very formal speeches – they merely talk, that is – and then Richard submits and the contest is over.

The great scenes of the play are not scenes of physical action: no actual fighting occurs on stage until Richard's murder in V.5. The scenes to which Shakespeare devoted most attention are static scenes, either of formal dignity (such as I.1 and I.3), or of emotional stress (III.2, V.1, the beginning of V.5), or of both (III.3, IV.1). The play concentrates upon those moments when people confront each other and strive to have their way by the force of their words – Henry and Mowbray (I.1), Gaunt and Richard (II.1), York and Henry (II.3), Henry and Richard (III.3). This preoccupation with argument and declamation comes to a climax in the spectacle of the Duke and Duchess of York each striving to sway Henry in opposite directions by the vehemence of their language (V.3).

There was sufficient material in Shakespeare's sources to have written a very different kind of play (see also Shakespeare's Use of Sources). For example, there is the intrigue and the ambush which resulted, according to Holinshed, in Richard being taken captive to Flint Castle: Shakespeare omits it all (see Commentary to III.3). Similarly, he leaves out the fighting of Richard's Irish campaign completely. The implication is that Shakespeare intentionally reduced the action as much as possible. When he did add to his sources, it was not to supply lively incidents but, in the scenes centred on the Queen (II.2, III.4, V.1), to allow himself to explore the **pathos** and sadness of Richard's situation.

TRAGEDY

The adjective 'tragic' is casually used in everyday speech to indicate that an event is very unfortunate. In literary discussion, and particularly with reference to drama, the word has a meaning both more precise and more elusive, denoting a text which generates a particular kind of response. Sadness is certainly part of that response, but only part. For the earliest, and much the most influential, discussion of that response, and of the nature of tragedy which generates it, we must turn to the ancient Greek philosopher Aristotle (384–322BC). In his *Poetics*, a treatise of aesthetic theory, he analysed the nature and effect of the tragedies of the Greek dramatists Sophocles, Aeschylus and Euripides. Aristotle's identification of a number of key aspects of dramatic tragedy, and the terms he used to describe them, have been standard features of all subsequent accounts of the genre. He argued that the plot of a tragedy should concern only a single, but significant, action; that its hero (Aristotle's ideas can equally be applied to heroines) should be a person of exceptional stature, who should undergo a reversal of fortune ('peripeteia' in Greek), brought about by his pride ('hubris') or error of judgement ('hamartia'); and that the hero should experience a moment of realisation or recognition of the truth of his situation ('anagnorisis'). Aristotle held that literature is mimetic – in other words, that it represents actual life – and that the powerful representation of the hero's tragic decline aroused in the audience feelings of sympathy, pity, awe and fear to the extent that they were purged or purified by the experience. For this experience Aristotle used the word 'catharsis'.

These ideas and terms have been extremely influential on all subsequent discussions of tragedy, particularly during the Renaissance and the eighteenth century, even though critics and commentators have never been able to agree exactly what Aristotle meant by them. Although

Shakespeare knew no Greek and certainly did not model his plays on the work of Greek dramatists, they can be applied helpfully to Shakespearean tragedy. His tragedies do evoke a sense of momentousness, as they deal with the fate of great figures in the state, with kings and princes whose deaths have repercussions throughout the kingdom. His **protagonists** are not only socially elevated; they are also figures of, if not exceptional talent or virtue, then exceptional presence and exceptional character. 'His legs bestrid the ocean; his reared arm / Crested the world' says Shakespeare's Cleopatra of Antony (*Antony and Cleopatra*, V.2.281–2), and there is something of that ability to dominate the action in all Shakespeare's tragic protagonists – Richard II has it, for all his self-pitying ruminations. Riven with faults though such figures are, with their death something fine or grand is lost. The effect of the tragedies is hence to induce a sense of waste, of lost potential. This is part of what might be called their cathartic effect. (In part due to the patriarchal structure of Renaissance society and the masculinist assumptions of its culture, such figures, in the work of Shakespeare and his fellow dramatists, were usually male. Shakespeare has only two tragic heroines, and both are coupled with men: Juliet in *Romeo and Juliet* and Cleopatra in *Antony and Cleopatra*.)

TRAGIC IRONY

It is typical of these **protagonists** that they misconstrue their situation, mistaking those around them (as Othello does Iago), or anticipating consequences that their actions will never bring about (as does Macbeth from the murder of Duncan), or failing to discern what is, to the audience, an all too obvious risk (as does Lear, when he gives up his authority). As a result, the audience is possessed of a greater understanding of the predicament than is granted the protagonist, foreseeing the outcome long before he or she does. So in *Richard II* the audience is ahead of Richard in realising that he quite mistakes the extent of his power and that he underestimates the threat posed by Henry. When he first appears, however, no vulnerability is apparent. This is typical of the genre: the tragic hero or heroine is first encountered at the height of his or her fortunes, apparently impervious to assault or decline, only to be brought to ruin and destruction, commonly as the result of a misconceived decision on his or her part. A man who is merely the victim of bad luck, whose fate is no fault of his own, is unlucky, but not tragic. On the other hand, a man who receives the punishment he deserves, who is wholly responsible for his fate, is justly, and not tragically, killed. A tragic fate is one which is both unlucky (the result of unfortunate circumstances) and deserved (the result of the protagonist's own failings). Recognising both that the character should die, and that he or she should not, the audience is left to wrestle with two irreconcilable reactions. That is the irony of tragedy and the tension characteristic of the tragic response.

Just such tragic irony and tension is to be encountered in *Richard II*. Richard is in many ways a corrupt and irresponsible ruler, and to that extent he deserves to lose his throne. On the other hand, it is not his fault that of all men he should have Henry Bolingbroke to deal with: it was, from Richard's point of view, very unlucky that he should choose to banish the one man determined enough to resist him. For that, of course, is Richard's tragic mistake, his moment of **hamartia**: he expects to solve all his difficulties by banishing Henry and Mowbray, and achieves quite the opposite result. However, even as he brings about his own destruction through this tragic miscalculation, the audience is increasingly aware both of the unattractiveness of Henry's new regime, and of the splendour – **rhetorical** and theatrical though it may have been – which had attended Richard's rule. A capable king would have been able to deal with Henry; indeed, a capable king would never have provoked him in the first place. Yet such a king would be as unlikely as Henry to haunt our memories as does Richard at Pomfret Castle.

TRAGIC INEVITABILITY

It is characteristic of Shakespearean tragedy that once the hero has made his fatal mistake the movement of the drama towards its tragic outcome grows increasingly inevitable. In *Richard II*, this effect is achieved in part through the presentation of Henry, who seems not to have to contrive his success actively, instead being carried along by good fortune. This sense of the characters' powerlessness over their destiny is enforced by the many references and **images** in the play which see the action as the inevitable working of fortune. One of the earliest indications of this comes from the Queen, just after Richard has left for Ireland (II.2.9–13):

> Yet again methinks
> Some unborn sorrow ripe in fortune's womb
> Is coming towards me, and my inward soul
> With nothing trembles. At something it grieves
> More than with parting from my lord the King.

A pregnant woman must give birth: the **image** suggests that the 'something' the Queen fears will – must – make itself known. Similarly, Green sees York's chances of withstanding Henry as nil (II.2.144–5):

> Alas, poor Duke! The task he undertakes
> Is numbering sands and drinking oceans dry.

York is clearly helpless to change the course of events. Richard himself uses a fatalistic image of inevitability: 'Down, down I come like glistering Phaethon' (III.3.178). Richard can no more resist Henry than Phaethon could withstand Zeus's thunderbolts. In the same way Richard's image of the water buckets in the deposition scene (IV.1.183–8) suggests that Henry's rise to power is inevitable, mechanical:

> Now is this golden crown like a deep well
> That owes two buckets, filling one another,
> The emptier ever dancing in the air,
> The other down, unseen, and full of water.
> That bucket down and full of tears am I,
> Drinking my griefs whilst you mount up on high.

As one bucket sinks, the other must necessarily rise.

TRAGIC LOSS

Lest we are in any danger of seeing Richard's fall not as tragic but as his just deserts for ruling badly, the play insists that, whatever justice Henry may claim on his side, when he does gain the throne something is lost. Richard, clearly, is a 'more kingly' king. Richard is inept and corrupt, certainly; Henry is far more efficient, but he is also duller. The England celebrated by Gaunt (II.1.31–58) will not have the same grandeur and romance under Henry. After all, his reign begins in Act IV with a very unseemly quarrel amongst his nobles, quite unlike the formal exchange of challenges (on the same issue, the death of Gloucester) which began the play. And Henry ends the play seeming suddenly aged, worried and guilt-ridden: there is no triumph here.

This impression is strengthened by the many references to Edward III and his sons. The Duchess of Gloucester sets the tone when she likens Edward's sons to 'seven vials of his sacred blood' (I.2.12). They were the true sons of a divinely appointed king. Repeatedly they are mentioned as a contrast in nobility, integrity and courage to the present times: they suggest England's glorious past (see, for example, York's recollection in II.3.98–104). When the play opens, only two, Gaunt and York, remain; after Gaunt's death, York is 'the last of noble Edward's sons' (II.1.171). We have a sense of a great family of princes dying out. Richard's behaviour betrays them, thus betrays his inheritance. This is Gaunt's charge at II.1.104–8 and York's later in the scene (lines 171–83).

With Richard's death all hope of recovering this nobility is lost. Richard was the last king to rule in direct succession from William the Conqueror: after him, the crown would go to the strongest. In other words, the fruitfulness of the Duchess's other **image** for Edward's sons, 'seven fair branches springing from one root' (I.2.13), has decayed: the tree withers and dies.

This sense of something irrecoverably lost is enforced by the many prophecies that, as a result of Richard's actions and Henry's usurpation of the throne, suffering and civil war will mark the future. Early in the play John of Gaunt casts himself in the role of a 'prophet new-inspired' to foretell that Richard's 'blaze of riot' will lead to disaster (II.1.31–9). Later in that scene, after Gaunt has died, his brother, the Duke of York, warns Richard that if he illegally seizes Henry's inheritance, 'You pluck a thousand dangers on your head' (line 205). The Welsh army awaiting Richard's return from Ireland is persuaded to disperse by a series of terrifying omens, 'signs' which 'forerun the death or fall of kings' (II.4.8–15). Then, after these repeated intimations of turmoil in the state, Richard, confronted by Henry at Flint Castle, evokes an appalling prospect of anarchy and bloodshed (III.3.93–100):

> He is come to open
> The purple testament of bleeding war;
> But ere the crown he looks for live in peace
> Ten thousand bloody crowns of mothers' sons

> Shall ill become the flower of England's face,
> Change the complexion of her maid-pale peace
> To scarlet indignation, and bedew
> Her pastor's grass with faithful English blood.

At the very moment of Richard's deposition, the Bishop of Carlisle gives still more graphic expression to the same foreboding (IV.1.134–44).

TRAGIC GAIN

For all the horror of the catastrophe, there is also an appropriateness about it which occasions something not unlike relief, almost an acknowledgement that the death of the hero is preferable to his survival. Unexpectedly, tragedy evokes a kind of exultation at the death of its hero, rather than despair, and sends its audience from the theatre with a positive, rather than a negative, experience. This is part of what is meant by Aristotle's term **catharsis**. The effect comes about partly because, as his worldly fortunes decline, the tragic hero grows in stature, coming, often, to a more secure understanding of the world which is destroying him. So Richard in Act V Scene 5 shows a new kind of self-knowledge and a new dignity in adversity; he experiences a kind of **anagnorisis**. He can now admit he has been wrong (V.5.41–9), when at the start of the play he had reacted with anger or incredulity to criticism (II.1.115–23, 186). He can now meditate on his sorrow without the emotional instability and excess he had shown in Act III Scene 2. In this respect, tragedy is not futile: the point should not be overstated, but there are ways in which Richard's suffering has been beneficial to him. There is also a sense that there would have been no future for Richard as the vassal of Henry. Far better that he should die a still glorious, if misguided, king, than that he should live on, doing what Henry tells him. That would amount to being less, not more, of a man than he is. Awful and dire though the tragic death is, it is also a relief and a release.

THEMES

Richard II is a play structured around a clear opposition, yet it is deeply ambivalent in its presentation of that opposition. Power is lost by one man and gained by another, yet the play does not allow the audience simply to admire the man who gains it and to condemn the man who loses it: too little is known about Henry and too much sympathy is felt for Richard. Equally, though, the audience cannot simply blame the man who gains it and respect the man who loses it: Henry has been too grievously wronged and Richard has committed too many extravagant and illegal acts. The audience is thus prevented from taking sides.

The principal theme of *Richard II* is kingship. Time and again characters discuss the rights and duties of a king and the rights and duties of a subject; yet the play refuses to choose between them. Its richness derives from the fact that, while it interrogates and analyses the positions adopted by the characters, Shakespeare declines to take a dogmatic or partisan line on the issues raised.

RICHARD'S MAJESTY

There is no disputing that there are dire failings in Richard. Gaunt (whose character is such that he is a reliable witness) directly implicates Richard in Gloucester's murder and later charges him with this (I.2.1–8, II.1.124–31). His brother York is of the same mind (II.1.165). We know of Richard's shortcomings as king (II.1.93–114, 163–70, III.4.48–66) and we see his despicable behaviour upon Henry's banishment and Gaunt's death (I.4, II.1.153–233).

Yet there is no doubt in the play but that Richard is the true king. Gaunt himself, more conscious of Richard's guilt and unworthiness than anyone else, refuses to act against him for this very reason (I.2.37–41):

> God's is the quarrel; for God's substitute,
>
> His deputy anointed in His sight,
>
> Hath caused his death; the which if wrongfully,
>
> Let heaven revenge, for I may never lift
>
> An angry arm against His minister.

Gaunt here expresses the predominant Tudor view of kingship: that a divinely appointed king is answerable only to God and cannot be challenged or judged by his subjects. To the Elizabethans, therefore, rebellion was a most heinous offence. The Bishop of Carlisle puts the

same point yet more strongly at the very moment that the King is about
to be deposed (IV.1.114–49; compare III.2.27–32, 36–62, 83–9, 97–101,
129–34; III.3.72–90). His intervention ensures that the audience is alive
to the enormity of what Henry is about to do.

Richard is always allowed majesty. York had remarked at Flint: 'Yet
looks he like a king' (III.3.68). In the deposition scene, the audience is
constantly reminded that a very grievous harm is being perpetrated
against Richard's majesty. This is especially so through Richard's
reference to the sufferings and trial of Christ. These bring together
several strands in Shakespeare's portrayal. Richard is a divinely appointed
king (as Christ's mission on earth was divinely ordained), betrayed by
those in whom he placed his trust (as Christ by Judas) and deposed by a
process which pretends to be legal while those responsible claim to be
innocent (as Christ was tried by Pilate). There can be no doubt about the
sanctity of Richard's kingship, nor that Shakespeare intended the
audience to share the Bishop of Carlisle's horror at the deposition.

HENRY'S WRONGS

On the other hand, there is no doubt that this same king wrongs Henry
grievously. He is seen doing so on stage, with a horrible callousness. The
prospect provokes York to make an impassioned plea to Richard. York
realises that if Richard seizes Henry's inheritance as Duke of Lancaster he
undermines the very foundations of society and dangerously weakens his
own position as king (II.1.195–9):

> Take Hereford's rights away, and take from Time
> His charters and his customary rights.
> Let not tomorrow then ensue today.
> Be not thyself; for how art thou a king
> But by fair sequence and succession?

Richard disregards this, and the warning that follows, with the wilful
blindness characteristic of his attitude earlier in the play, but the audience
cannot disregard it. Just as Shakespeare gave full weight to the sanctity of
Richard's kingship, so he gives full weight to the grievance which
provokes Henry. The recklessness of Richard's act is underscored by its
positioning in Act II Scene 2 between the last moments of Gaunt, who

dies warning Richard against his folly, and York's plea to him to reconsider. Its criminal insensitivity is heightened by the fact that it is targeted against Gaunt's son and heir; and its political ineptitude is demonstrated by the stirrings of rebellion which immediately follow in the exchange with Northumberland. It is not coincidence that in these very passages Shakespeare chooses to remind us of Edward III (II.1.124–38, 171–83). The point is clear: Richard is betraying the nobility of the Plantagenet kings.

Furthermore, Henry, though a reticent figure, never behaves with the pettiness or meanness of Richard. He has a confident authority. He can grant Aumerle a pardon in Act V Scene 3 (unlike Richard in Act I Scenes 1 and 3, Henry is not implicated in the guilt of his nobles). Shakespeare could have discredited Henry's position by presenting him as vengeful and unscrupulous, but this is not the case: there is scope to believe that Henry never wished Richard to be murdered, and he certainly never knew of, or actively arranged, the crime. Richard regards Henry's popular following with scorn (I.4.23–36), but it does not seem contemptible to an audience – on the contrary, it is Richard's scorn which is contemptible. Richard ignores his subjects; secure in his divine right, he does not need their favour and seems to have no sense that he owes it to them to rule in their interest. Henry does pay attention to others, to common people, and (whatever we may know to the contrary) deserves their admiration. Certainly, it is the people's esteem for Henry which renders Richard's position hopeless (III.2.112–20).

THE CENTRAL DILEMMA

There is, then, right and wrong on both sides: on the one hand the divinely appointed king who ignores his people; on the other, the man of justice who enjoys popular support but who has no claim to the throne. It is in this respect that York is so significant in the play. In him is represented exactly this dilemma, as we see at II.2.111–15:

> Both are my kinsmen.
> T'one is my sovereign, whom both my oath
> And duty bids defend. T'other again
> Is my kinsman, whom the King hath wronged,
> Whom conscience and my kindred bids to right.

As York here despairs of reconciling these competing claims, so the play recognises both the authority of Richard's kingship and Richard's failings, both the wrongs Henry sustains and the injustice of what he does to Richard. The play does not categorically conclude either that a king should not be judged or that Henry was right to act against Richard.

If there is a final verdict in *Richard II*, it is that the affair is a mystery providentially guided. The plotting of the action lends an effortless ease to events, so that they hardly seem to depend upon human causation at all; Richard appears in the later scenes as the victim of circumstances he is powerless to prevent; and the play's figurative language constantly raises **images** of the inevitability of the action. All this supports York's verdict: 'But heaven hath a hand in these events' (V.2.37).

STYLE

WORDPLAY

Richard II is the work of a poet alive to the ambiguities of words, to their proliferation of different senses – sometimes called 'plurisignation' (having many senses and associations), 'multivocality' (speaking with many voices, and so susceptible of many interpretations) or 'polysemy' (having many meanings). The text delights in the dexterous manipulation of these meanings. The comic use of puns and quibbles is familiar, but verbal ingenuity at moments of serious drama may disconcert modern readers who prefer in literary style the straightforward and direct over the elaborate and ingenious. Unusually for a Shakespeare play, *Richard II* has no comic interludes, but in nearly every scene it revels in **semantic** games and **rhetorical** figures. A conspicuous example occurs early on when the dying Gaunt puns on his name (II.1.72–83). This is ingenious, and it does stress Gaunt's age and anguish, but its playful quality appears at odds with the sincere expression of feeling. Yet Shakespeare actually signals this ingenuity when he has Richard exclaim 'Can sick men play so nicely with their names?' (II.1.84).

This is a **self-reflexive** moment which alerts the audience to the linguistic playfulness of the drama's own text. The implication is that both Shakespeare and his Elizabethan audience savoured such rhetorical dexterity for its inventiveness and ingenuity, or for what the period would have called its 'wit'. In modern English this word suggests little more than a joke, but in Elizabethan English (though the absurd and the comic might be involved) it suggested the combination of intellectual and artistic adroitness required for the novel, unexpected, pointed and provocative manipulation of an idea or **image**. It was a quality greatly prized – much of the effect of the poetry of Shakespeare's contemporary John Donne, for example, derives from the outrageousness and preposterousness of his witty development of ideas. It leads to a fondness for puns, ambiguity, semantic puzzles, paradoxical and aphoristic statements, and for improbable combinations of ideas or images.

A case in point occurs when Richard submits to Henry. At this dire moment in his fortunes, a pun answers to Richard's sense of his ignoble situation (III.3.178–81):

> Down, down I come like glistering Phaethon,
> Wanting the manage of unruly jades.
> In the base-court – base-court, where kings grow base
> To come at traitors' calls, and do them grace.

Here, a common technical term ('base-court', meaning lower, or ground-level, court) becomes suggestive of the moral treachery which is taking place ('where kings grow base'), so that Richard's actual descent from the walls of Flint Castle becomes an action **symbolising** his descent from high and noble office to ignominy and shame.

Rhyme

In Renaissance drama, **prose** was commonly employed for comic scenes and for characters of low social standing. With its concentration upon court intrigue and action of high seriousness, *Richard II* makes no use of prose. It has no equivalent to the Boar's Head scenes in the *Henry IV* plays, the gravedigger scene in *Hamlet* (Act V Scene 1) or the porter scene in *Macbeth* (Act II Scene 3). Its poetic character is sustained by the use throughout of **blank verse**, with the frequent introduction of rhyme. Two lines from the Bishop of Carlisle's prophetic speech in Act IV (lines 137–8) illustrate this:

> The blood of English shall manure the ground,
> And future ages groan for this foul act.

Here, every second syllable is stressed. Unrelieved, such regularity could become very monotonous: Shakespeare introduces a good deal of variety (that is, modulation) in his stress patterns, though the **iambic pentameter** base is always the controlling pattern. This prevents the text from ever lapsing into the unpredictable rhythm of **prose**.

The frequent use of rhyme still further distances the play's medium from everyday speech. Rhyme is a more overtly artificial medium than **blank verse**, its echoing sounds calling attention to its manipulation of words. It also, of course, highlights the particular words which rhyme. Rhyme can thus act as a signal to the audience, for example, that a scene has ended (e.g. the final two lines of Act II Scene 4 or Act III Scene 4), or to mark an exit (e.g. Richard's exit at I.3.247–8). It underscores a significant moment, such as a leave-taking (e.g. York's parting from Richard at II.1.211–14), and, used at length, it can stress the formality and ritualistic quality of a scene (e.g. I.1.158–205). It is also used to stress a point, as, for example, it gives emphasis to Henry's denunciation of Mowbray at I.1.41–6.

Rhyme is used, too, to conclude a **blank verse** speech with emphasis (e.g. I.2.54–5), to insist that a statement allows no contradiction, and to give a statement an aphoristic or proverbial turn of phrase (e.g. II.1.7–8). When rhyme sounds echo between characters, even though they may be disagreeing, it serves to link what they are saying and so underlines the fact that in some way they depend upon each other's reactions. The interdependence of the fortunes of Richard and Henry is linguistically captured when, to Henry's 'I thought you had been willing to resign', Richard replies 'My crown I am; but still my griefs are mine', thus completing the **couplet** (IV.1.189–90). Similarly, Henry's apparently considerate, but certainly specious, expression of concern, 'Part of your cares you give me with your crown', is brushed aside by Richard's reply, 'Your cares set up do not pluck my cares down' (IV.1.193–4).

Monologues

The recurrent use of rhyme (see above) also ensures that the audience is constantly aware of the poetic nature of the play. *Richard II* is a play which calls attention to the artifice and ingenuity of its language. This feature is most marked in the frequent long speeches. With so little physical action in the play (see Plot & Structure), the centre of interest lies in what the characters say. As if to sustain this interest, what they say often has the character not of a contribution to an ongoing debate but of a self-sufficient utterance, of a speech detached from the drama of the play. There is only one real **soliloquy**, at the beginning of Act V Scene 5, but, despite the text's appearance of dialogue, the exchanges between its characters are often suspended for the delivery of long speeches of twenty or thirty lines which, although supposedly addressed to another character on stage, in fact have the quality of soliloquies. The dynamic of such speeches lies in their exploration of inner thoughts or in the self-preoccupied development of an **image** or idea, rather than in communication with another character. Gaunt's 'England' speech in II.1.31–68 is an example, which develops its image of England at far greater length than is required by the attempt to induce Richard to reform. Richard's speeches in Act III Scene 2 are another case in point: these are not intended to persuade anyone to a course of action. In the deposition scene, Richard is not really engaged in dialogue. Though the stage is filled with courtiers, his speech to the mirror (IV.1.275–90) is a private meditation. And even when characters are intent on persuasion through argument, it is declamation rather than conversation that we hear: examples are Gaunt's rebukes to Richard (II.1.93–114, 124–38), Henry's account to York of his aims (II.3.112–35), and the Bishop of Carlisle's address (IV.1.114–49).

IMAGERY

To its employment of rhyme and its delight in linguistic ingenuity, *Richard II* adds an exceptional **metaphorical** richness. Typically, this **imagery** is evocative, sensual, luxuriant and exotic. It adds greatly to the emotional power of the play, to the audience's sense of the richness of Richard's world. In particular, the play makes use of a small group of recurrent images. Through these image clusters the play returns again and again to key concepts and **motifs**. The repeated references to blood, for example, remind us of the cruelty and treachery that are not very far from the splendid world of Richard's court. The many **allusions** to

Edward III and his sons (often linked with the blood imagery, as when
the Duchess of Gloucester refers to Edward's seven sons as 'seven vials of
his sacred blood', I.2.12) prevent us from forgetting the Plantagenet
nobility betrayed by Richard. **Images** of youth and age underline
Richard's inexperience – York would have his brother Gaunt 'Deal mildly
with his youth' (II.1.69) – but images of death and the grave also haunt
the play, darkening its atmosphere. Richard in despair wishes to 'talk of
graves, of worms, and epitaphs' (III.2.145), while the Bishop of Carlisle
foresees that 'The blood of English shall manure the ground' and that
England will become like Golgotha, that place of death (IV.1.137, 144).

One of the richest of these recurrent **images** is that of the sun. This
is a particularly appropriate image, since the sun formed part of Richard's
own badge. Shakespeare uses it to suggest the splendour of Richard's
kingship and, since the sun is the most important body in the sky and
its light a traditional image for God's grace, his conception of the divinity
of a king. Richard's almost mystical, and wholly unrealistic, sense of
his royal nature is evident when, confronted with bad news in Act III
Scene 2, he compares his unassailable power as king with the dominance
of the sun in the sky, and foresees himself 'rising in our throne, the east',
shaming Henry, who will not be able 'to endure the sight of day'
(III.2.36–53). But when he comes to submit to Henry, it is with a very
different sun image on his lips: 'Down, down I come like glistering
Phaeton' (III.3.178).

Language & self-reflexivity

In many of his plays Shakespeare discusses language and its powers.
Richard II is no exception. Its characters are fully aware of both the
influence and the deceptiveness of words, and of their importance to civil
and to human life: Mowbray sees his banishment in terms of loss of the
occasion to use English (I.3.159–73); Gaunt's death is reported by
Northumberland as a loss of words, 'His tongue is now a stringless
instrument' (II.1.149). Henry calls attention to the power of a king's
words (I.3.213–15) and Richard's loss of power is seen when he has to eat
his own kingly words (III.3.133–6). But if words can sway, they can also
deceive: the Duchess of York does not believe her husband to be sincere
in demanding Aumerle's death (V.3.101), and York himself points to the

false words of Richard's favourites (II.1.17–26). Words are limited, too – we are reminded that they cannot express the deepest feelings when the faithful groom says to Richard: 'What my tongue dares not, that my heart shall say' (V.5.97). As that line suggests, they are also dangerous things: Ross is afraid to speak his mind (II.1.228–9) and the Abbot of Westminster swears the conspirators to silence (IV.1.327–8).

It is, at times, as if the characters are themselves aware that they are part of a literary work, that they are part of a story. They can call attention to details of literary technique: for example, Richard begins his **soliloquy** at Pomfret by explaining the **metaphorical** method he has adopted: 'I have been studying how I may compare / This prison where I live unto the world' (V.5.1–2). More often, they liken their experiences to those of fictional characters. Gaunt speaks of his 'death's sad tale' (II.1.16), Richard sees himself as like those kings whose deaths are recounted in 'sad stories' (III.2.156), and he speaks of kings as mere actors playing a part (III.2.160–70). On his way to imprisonment he sees his life as a 'lamentable tale' (V.1.44), and his murderer speaks of his crime as 'chronicled in hell' (V.5.116). York tells his wife 'the story' of Richard and Henry's entrance into London (V.2.1–3). Such remarks are typical of the **self-reflexive** theatricality of Renaissance drama; the characters speaking are indeed fictional, and the persons speaking are indeed actors. At such moments, the drama declares its own textuality, its fabrication of reality. In this particular play, however, such comments also contribute to the impression that its action is a mysterious 'pageant' (IV.1.320) in which people play the part providentially assigned to them, until they are claimed by the 'antic' Death (III.2.162).

CHARACTERISATION

Richard II is focused on two figures: Henry and Richard. They have contrasting characters, but, while it has psychological persuasiveness and is, to a degree, a study in conflicting temperaments, the play is fascinated just as much by the alternative political regimes which are centred on these men – how they exercise power, for what ends and with what promise for the future. Quite dissimilar in their sense of their own identities and in their self-presentation, the two are different too in the way they engage with events: it could almost be said that while Richard reacts, Henry acts.

With Richard are associated his 'flatterers', the 'caterpillars of the commonwealth' (II.3.165, III.4.40–7): Bushy, Bagot and Green. These characters are not individualised but serve to represent those favourites who, in the opinion of his critics, have misled Richard (II.1.100, 241–2; III.1.8–10). All that is necessary for the play is that they should be young (like Richard himself), unpleasant (Richard's callous behaviour in I.4 must be familiar and acceptable to them) and unheroic (as they are in II.2.122–48), divorced from the audience's sympathy when they come to be executed in III.1. With them is linked Aumerle (see I.4), but he is a more fully realised character, loyal to Richard until the discovery of the Abbot of Westminster's plot in Act V. Contrasted with these unattractive figures are the wise old counsellor, Gaunt, the staunch Bishop of Carlisle, and the Queen, for whom Richard is primarily a man, not a king. For his courtiers, Richard is only a source of wealth and influence, whom they desert as soon as the going gets rough.

Henry has fewer followers; indeed, only two of any note: the bluff Earl of Northumberland, who has little patience with Richard's elaborate speeches and high-strung emotions, and his son, Harry Percy, whose vigorous youth contrasts with the rather weak immaturity which Richard himself at times displays. However, with the down-to-earth character of Henry, these two are sufficient to give Henry's party (the Lancastrians) the appearance of being composed of no-nonsense, practical and sturdy people, unlike Richard's unstable and flighty followers.

These two groups are linked by York, the uncle of both Richard and Henry, who, in the course of the play, changes his allegiance from the one to the other.

HENRY

In one sense, Henry Bolingbroke is the hero of the play. It is he who successfully supplants Richard as king, to rule as Henry IV. And yet he is a strangely elusive hero, one about whom it is difficult to form a view – we hardly know Henry at all. He speaks well and imposingly in Scenes 1 and 3 of Act I, but also very formally. His desire to avenge Gloucester's death may be disinterested, but it may equally well be a calculated and self-interested political move. Neither he nor anyone else discloses his motives. He is a character without a personal or inner life. When Richard banishes him, Henry replies simply, 'Your will be done' (I.3.144). There is no evidence of surprise, shock or dismay (contrast this with Mowbray's reaction at I.3.154–73). This is characteristic of Henry throughout the play: he says very little, and never anything about his own innermost thoughts and feelings. Richard, it seems, suspects Henry of ambition right from the start (see I.1.109, I.3.129–32) but Henry, when he returns from banishment, insists that he comes only to gain his rights as Duke of Lancaster (II.3.112–35). York recognises the justness of Henry's claim (II.1.187–99, II.2.111–15, II.3.140–1), but he also soon comes to suspect Henry of aiming at more than this (III.3.16–17). Henry similarly tells Richard at Flint Castle that he wants only his ducal rights (III.3.31–61), but Richard remains convinced that Henry is not telling the truth, and foresees his own deposition (III.3.143–59). Despite all this suspicion, however, we hear nothing from Henry himself about his real intentions. His first (and last) reference to the crown is the single, abrupt line in which he actually takes it: 'In God's name I'll ascend the regal throne' (IV.1.113). Whether this was what Henry always intended, or whether the ambition grew gradually, we cannot know: the text offers no reliable indication of just when he conceives this higher aim. Similarly, Henry says nothing of how he justifies his claim to the throne, what he supposes his title is, nor of what, as king, he intends to do. Silence surrounds Henry's plans as impenetrably as his motives.

With this reticence goes an extraordinary ease of accomplishment (see also Plot & Structure). Henry seems to have to make no effort at all to organise an invasion, win support, or capture the King. At the end of Act III Scene 1 he expects to fight the Welsh, but we know from Act II Scene 4 that they have disbanded. Even Henry himself is surprised to find Richard at Flint so easily (III.3.20–6). Shakespeare has deliberately arranged it so that he stumbles upon the King, whereupon Richard simply 'comes down' (III.3.178).

This has two effects. First, the character of Henry is not in itself very engaging: his inner life is insufficiently developed to sustain close scrutiny or, in the theatre, to arouse strong feelings. We simply do not know enough about him. Towards the end of the play, there are signs of anxiety (V.3.1–12) and guilt (V.6.45–52), but these come after the taking of the throne. In the body of the play, it is Richard, not Henry, who commands attention.

Second, Henry seems not to be directing events at all. Because Shakespeare tells us so little about his plans and intentions it seems that he has none, and consequently he appears to be someone for whom everything goes right by remarkably good fortune. He simply lands in England, and the crown falls into his lap. (See also Tragic Inevitability.)

RICHARD

With so taciturn a rival, Richard holds centre stage at the emotional and psychological heart of the play. Though he is deposed, his centrality in the play remains far more secure than, for example, that of Henry IV in Shakespeare's two subsequent history plays (see *Richard II* and Shakespeare's History Plays). This centrality is achieved in part by the allocation of textual space: Richard says a very great deal. However, what Richard says is as important as how much he says. Though he is a king, what he talks about is less often the public realm than it is the private sphere of his own feelings and emotions. Where Henry is directorial, peremptory, imperative and active, Richard is reflective, introspective, meditative and passive, as he ponders his predicament in long speeches which are personal reveries rather than addresses to the other persons on the stage. If Henry's inner life is among the most restrained of any of Shakespeare's leading figures, Richard's is among the richest.

It is this which in large part prompts a sympathetic response to Richard's fate; but the order in which Shakespeare reveals features of his character is still more important in winning sympathy. The audience's view of Richard passes through three stages, as follows.

THE REGAL, BUT DUPLICITOUS, MONARCH (I.1–I.3)
The monarch is, above all, the source of law and order, and it is fulfilling this role that Richard is introduced in Act I Scene 1. In dealing with the quarrel between Henry Bolingbroke and Thomas Mowbray he speaks royally and powerfully. He appears to be, as he says, impartial (I.1.115–23) and authoritative, for when he orders the appellants to appear at Coventry he is obeyed (I.1.196–201). However, before the

scene at Coventry, Act I Scene 2 intervenes and it very seriously qualifies the favourable impression Richard has made. From Gaunt we learn that Richard himself was involved in Gloucester's murder, the subject of the quarrel in the first scene. Far from being an impartial judge removed from the question at issue, Richard is himself implicated in it.

Richard is not, however, involved merely as a guilty party. At I.1.104 Henry says that Gloucester's blood ran 'like sacrificing Abel's'. In the Bible Abel was killed by his brother Cain, and the **image** suggests a close relationship between murderer and victim – Gloucester was, of course, Richard's uncle. Thus what seems like a stately and ceremonial occasion is, in fact, a family quarrel. Henry's grandfather Edward III is Richard's grandfather, and Richard's roundabout way of saying 'cousin' ('father's brother's son', line 117) only draws attention to the nearness of their relationship. In Act I Scene 1 an accusation is made by one cousin before another cousin of the murder of an uncle, a crime for which, we learn in Act I Scene 2, the adjudicating cousin was himself responsible. The distinctions between ruler and ruled, monarch and subject, judge and accused, which the regal formalities seek to establish, are subverted: this king is not at all detached from the events on which he sits in judgement. While the ritual proclaims security, this is an insecure monarch who must resort to duplicity. It is perhaps for this reason that Richard already suspects Henry's motives and imagines him to be after the throne.

Richard's involvement in the quarrel may explain why in Act I Scene 3 he abruptly stops the contest and banishes both Henry and Mowbray. Each poses a threat to him: Mowbray knows the truth about Richard's involvement and is therefore dangerous (and he does seem very hurt by Richard's sentence, I.3.154–73); on the other hand, Richard continues to entertain suspicion of Henry's ambition (I.3.129–32), which he will voice again in the next scene (I.4.20–36). By banishing both, he hopes to prevent Mowbray from revealing what he knows and to preserve himself from Henry's aspiration to the throne.

THE TYRANT (I.4–II.1)
The misgivings which have followed the introduction of Richard as a public and regal figure are strengthened when he is presented in private conversation with his close friends in Act I Scene 4. There is not now the pressure of Scenes 1 and 3 of Act I to put on a public performance, to act

the King, and the result is a dismaying comedown. Richard appears petulant, resentful, callous, even prepared to act illegally to finance his Irish campaign. This revelation of Richard's private character prepares the audience to believe the criticisms levelled at him by Gaunt in the next scene (Act II Scene 1); and when, on Gaunt's death, Richard seizes his wealth and lands, all the suspicions that have been gathered are confirmed. Richard is a king without any of Gaunt's or York's sense of duty. He flouts the law and ignores criticism, with total disregard for the consequences. He acknowledges no bond between King and subject; thinks he can banish Henry without consequence; supposes he may farm his realm without any comeback; and robs Gaunt with impunity. Gaunt had tried to warn him that such deeds were storing up trouble for the future (II.1.95–9), but in vain. When York's outburst actually shows Richard the effect his illegal actions have on loyal subjects, Richard is simply unable to grasp what is wrong: 'Why, uncle, what's the matter?' he asks (II.1.186). It is this inability to see what is the matter which gives Henry his easy road to the throne, for Richard has alienated all those upon whom he depends to oppose any threat to his crown. He fails to realise that, however absolute and immutable a king's title to the throne, his hold over his people is not unconditional. Effective rule requires their loyalty and support, and that has to be earned.

THE WRONGED KING (III.2–V.5)
By the time Richard sets off for Ireland, the play has thus adduced ample evidence that he is a corrupt and tyrannical ruler. During the following scenes the consequences are evident as Henry easily gains the allegiance of people who feel no affection or loyalty to their king (the point is made repeatedly: I.4.20–36; II.1.246–8; III.2.112–20). During most of this process, Richard is absent from the stage. This, of course, contributes to our sense of the ease of Henry's progress (there is no monarch to oppose him), but it also ensures that when Richard returns in Act III Scene 2 it has been some while since the audience directly experienced his malevolence and abuse of power. Equally, the audience very well knows what Richard is about to discover: that his position is hopeless. The effect of this structural arrangement is to separate the guilty king of the early scenes from the suffering king of the later part of the play. Drama works through time: the evidence of Richard's failings, which explains his

loss of power, now fades as, powerless, Richard is presented as the victim of circumstances. Deprived of the scope to rule, Richard is deprived also of the scope to continue his misrule. He can thus now appear in an altogether more sympathetic light. A number of features of the later scenes contribute to this construction of a figure who can engage the audience sympathetically and ensure that, in the last scenes of the play, Richard has no rival for the audience's attention or compassion:

- With Richard's culpability confined to the beginning of the play, his maladministration is now rarely mentioned (he does not confess publicly in Act IV as Northumberland demands). Recollections of his guilt do not complicate responses to his suffering.
- That suffering is constantly before us as Richard repeatedly explores his agony of mind and spirit. His mental turmoil is the matter of his speeches in III.2, III.3, IV.1, V.1 and V.5, and so it is his state of mind, and no longer his failings as king, which commands attention.
- Because Richard's guilt is now in the background, he appears as the victim of rebellion and betrayal. This is certainly his own view, which he presents by likening Henry and his followers to Judas Iscariot and Pontius Pilate.
- Richard is accorded exceptionally evocative and haunting poetry in which to express himself, so that his thoughts and feelings are conveyed to us far more movingly than those of anyone else.

The portrayal of Richard has thus been contrived both to allow that he was a culpable and negligent ruler and to generate a sympathetic response to him. It would not quite be accurate to say either that Richard is a tyrant who deserves to lose his throne or that he is an appealing figure who is cruelly and unjustly treated. He is both – or, to put it another way, he is a **tragic** hero.

GAUNT

John of Gaunt, Duke of Lancaster, appears in only four scenes of the play, dying in Act II Scene 1, but he plays a significant role in the scheme of the drama. He is an old man, a link with the great King Edward III, his father: in Gaunt lives the noble tradition of England's glorious past. Richard's scornful and derisive attitude to Gaunt (I.4.59–64, II.1.115–23) thus demonstrates how little respect he pays to his heritage.

In these early scenes of the play, Gaunt voices criticism of Richard which is totally disinterested. That is the crucial point: Henry has a grievance against Richard and can be expected to oppose the King out of self-interest. Gaunt, however, is prepared to put aside personal feelings when trying to do what is best for his country – for example, though as a father he bitterly regrets it, as a counsellor he agrees to the banishment of his son because he believes it to be in the interest of peace in England (I.3.233–46). He speaks against Richard not out of personal malice but out of concern for the political well-being of his country. His famous speech in II.1.31–68 serves to conjure up in the minds of the audience early in the play a vision of England as an especially blessed land, a vision which has a lasting effect upon the audience's view of the action and of Richard's misdeeds. And Gaunt is constant in his opposition to the King's wrongdoings. Not only is he prepared to go to his death trying to reform the King, but, we gather from II.1.15, he has spent the earlier years of the King's reign in the same endeavour.

Yet such is Gaunt's commitment to his duty (as he sees it) that he refuses to act against Richard himself, although he feels deeply the injustice of the murder of his brother Gloucester (I.2.1–8, 37–41). It is not for him to try to dethrone God's appointed deputy on earth. Unlike his son, Henry, he will place his trust in God to right matters; unlike his brother, York, however, he will resolutely and fearlessly oppose what he sees as the King's neglect of his duty; and, unlike his nephew, Richard, he will put the good of England before all else. In these ways he offers a model of nobility against which to measure the other characters in the play, all of whom are found wanting.

YORK

Edmund of Langley, Duke of York, is Gaunt's brother and the last of Edward III's sons. He is both like and unlike his brother. He is like him in his absolute commitment to his duty. Richard recognises this loyalty – just after York has rebuked him passionately and left the stage in disgust, he still makes the Duke Governor of England in his absence (II.1.220–1). Later in the play, when York has taken an oath of allegiance to the new King Henry IV, he maintains his loyalty to Henry even to the point of informing on his own son Aumerle (V.3.53–72). It is no surprise that Henry sees in his uncle York something of his own father Gaunt (II.3.112–21), for York, like Gaunt, lets neither family nor personal considerations come before duty.

Yet York is a much less commanding figure than Gaunt. For York old age means not (as for Gaunt) the wisdom of experience and the courage of resolution. On the contrary, it means weakness, indecision and helplessness. It is York himself who tries to dissuade Gaunt from criticising the King lest it do more harm than good (II.1.3–4, 17–30) and, though he does make some efforts to organise resistance to Henry, these efforts are rather half-hearted (II.2.98–121). When York confronts Henry, he simply admits he is powerless and yields (II.3.151–6). He is a man with neither natural authority nor initiative. Affairs simply leave him confused. So, from being Richard's governor, he comes to claim to be neutral (II.3.157–8). He feels sympathy for Richard (III.3.68–71), but by the time of the deposition he has moved from his neutrality to Henry's side and is the first to hail the new king (IV.1.107–12). By V.2.39 he has taken an oath of allegiance to Henry IV. It seems that, for all his sense of duty, he drifts with – or is pushed by – events. The impression is of a man unable to cope: 'Things past redress are now with me past care' (II.3.170).

York's indecision and ineffectuality constitute a crucial part of the design of *Richard II*, for in him is seen the central dilemma of the play (see also Themes); Gaunt dies before having to face this dilemma. York has outlived his time: his simple but firm sense of duty, ideal when the King is strong and noble like Edward III, does not know which way to turn when the King is weak and negligent like Richard II. It is precisely because York both wants to remain loyal to Richard and recognises that he has not behaved as a king should towards Henry that he is caught between the two sides (II.2.111–15). We might say that in him we see the confusion that results when the King ceases to be the true ruler and inspiration of his people.

A UMERLE

Edward of York, Duke of Aumerle, might appear to be made of sterner stuff than his father, the Duke of York. He refutes the charge of being involved in Gloucester's murder with courage and defiance (IV.1.8–85). He is prepared to take part in the Abbot of Westminster's plot to restore

Richard to the throne (IV.1.323–4), and so does seem to have a stronger commitment to the old king than his father does. On the other hand, his behaviour in I.4.1–19, where he speaks sneeringly of Henry after having seemed to behave affectionately to him in I.3.249–50, places him in the company of Richard's vindictive followers. And when the Abbot's plot is discovered by York, he is ready enough to take his mother's advice and seek Henry's pardon (V.2.112–14, V.3.29–31). In just the same way, Richard's other companions try to save their own skins when in danger. Aumerle is a loyal, but not very noble, adherent of Richard's party.

NORTHUMBERLAND

Henry Percy, Earl of Northumberland, typifies Henry's followers as Aumerle does Richard's. He is practical, efficient and down-to-earth. At the end of Act II Scene 1 he has full knowledge of Henry's preparations for invasion and is resolute in acting quickly to join him. It is from him (as York notices) that we get the first hint that there is a lack of respect for Richard's kingship amongst Henry's adherents (III.3.5–17). He has little patience with Richard's long speeches in the deposition scene and is concerned to prevent Richard from presenting himself as a martyr by having him confess publicly his crimes (IV.1.221–71). It is the same disregard for high sentiment which enables him promptly to arrest the Bishop of Carlisle after his speech in defence of Richard (IV.1.150–3). Northumberland is not a man to be swayed from his purpose by either exhibitions of emotional suffering or idealistic arguments about duty. In this respect, he typifies the no-nonsense approach of Henry and his party. This man of affairs is an excellent foil both to Richard's hopelessly inept idealism and to York's weak irresolution.

Richard calls him the 'ladder' by which Henry ascends to the throne (V.1.55). Although Shakespeare pays little attention to the details of Henry's rise, we can trace the steps Northumberland takes on his behalf:
• he rallies the lords to side with Henry (II.1.224–300)
• he accompanies Henry after he has landed at Ravenspurgh (II.3)
• he executes Richard's favourites on Henry's orders (III.1.35)
• at Flint Castle he is Henry's envoy to Richard (III.3.31–4, 101–20, 142, 176–7)

- he arrests the Bishop of Carlisle and tries to make Richard confess his crimes (IV.1.150–3, 221–71)
- he sends Richard to Pomfret and the Queen to France (V.1.52–5)
- he successfully breaks up the conspiracy against Henry (V.6.6–10)

In short, no one is more active on Henry's behalf than Northumberland; no one is more single-minded in carrying through a plan. Yet no one is more dangerous as an ally, for, with his insensitivity to questions of conscience, morality and loyalty ('My guilt be on my head, and there an end' is how he abruptly dismisses them in V.1.69), Northumberland can hardly be trusted. It is no surprise to find that, as Richard prophesies (V.1.55–68), in the *Henry IV* plays he rebels against Henry when he finds it in his interest to do so.

B ISHOP OF CARLISLE

Thomas Merke, Bishop of Carlisle, is the noblest of Richard's followers, absolutely dedicated to his king. He is prepared to defend Richard in the midst of the enemy camp in Act IV and to fight to restore him to his throne (IV.1.320–33, V.6.19–23). Despite his part in the Abbot of Westminster's plot, Henry, his enemy, grants him his life (V.6.24–7), but it seems unlikely his unwavering commitment would ever have allowed him, like Aumerle, to change his allegiance and beg for a pardon. Henry does nevertheless pardon him because, as he says, 'High sparks of honour in thee have I seen' (V.6.29). There is similar evidence of his holiness and dignity earlier in the play when Percy says that there is in Flint Castle with Richard 'a clergyman of holy reverence', and from this description Northumberland recognises the Bishop (III.3.27–30). To this bishop Shakespeare gives the most eloquent defence of Richard's inalienable rights as divinely anointed king (IV.1.114–31), but he also advises Richard to take steps to defend himself (III.2.27–32). Clearly, the Bishop is not an ecclesiastic ignorant of the ways of the world. He believes that 'heaven helps those who help themselves' (and he himself acts in the plot against Henry). That it is this high-minded clergyman, so unlike Richard's flatterers and the brusque Earl of Northumberland, who foretells bloody civil war as the consequence of Richard's deposition, lends the prophecy an awful authority (IV.1.132–49).

QUEEN ISABEL

In the theatre of Shakespeare's day female roles were played by boys. This does not seem to have restricted Shakespeare much in the conception of his female characters – Rosalind in *As You Like It*, Beatrice in *Much Ado About Nothing* and Cleopatra in *Antony and Cleopatra* remain amongst the most challenging and rewarding parts for actresses in the dramatic repertoire. There is, however, a recurrent kind of female character in his plays, which may owe something to the fact that only boys were available to play female roles. This is the figure of a beautiful young woman of innocence and simplicity. It is not a character with great range, and so does not demand too much of its performer. In the **tragedies**, this character, caught up in a situation she is powerless to influence, becomes a passive figure of **pathos** such are Ophelia in *Hamlet* and Desdemona in *Othello*.

The Queen in *Richard II* belongs in this company. She has a gentleness which contrasts with Richard's heartless attitude to Gaunt (II.1.71) and a simplicity which can hope that the cruel world of power politics might yet allow her to stay with Richard after his fall (V.1.83–7). As Richard says, 'That were some love, but little policy' (V.1.84). Hers is a world of love: the world of Henry and Northumberland a world of expedient policy.

To that latter world she is a marginal figure, able only to catch occasional glimpses of its rivalries and plots, never able fully to understand its machinations. Helplessness is her condition. In Act II Scene 2 she fearfully anticipates something dreadful in the future which she cannot understand because she is excluded from the world of men. In Act III Scene 4 she overhears from another that Richard is in Henry's power. In Act V Scene 1, at the end of it all, she comes to see again the husband whose fortunes she has had no part in. She is a **choric** figure: in these scenes, by exploring her emotions, Shakespeare deepens our sense of the **pathos** and **tragedy** of what happens to Richard. He creates a tender and loving relationship (to achieve which he has deliberately made the Queen older than her eleven years in 1399). In her, what happens to Richard is registered by one who loves him as a man, more dearly and intimately than anyone loves him as King. That she should so cry out, in haunting and evocative lines, at the change in him, deepens awareness of what he has suffered (V.1.8–15), just as her earlier experience of a 'nameless woe' increased the audience's apprehension (II.2.1–40).

PERCY

Northumberland's son Harry Percy will, as 'Hotspur', play a large part in *Henry IV Part 1*, but his role in *Richard II* is slight. Our main impression is of a vigorous and brave young man, full of promise and far more purposeful (II.3.41–4) than either Richard's followers or the son Henry mentions at the beginning of Act V Scene 3 – this is the Prince Hal who will be Harry Percy's rival in *Henry IV Part 1* and will eventually become Henry V.

PART FOUR

Textual Analysis

TEXT 1   GAUNT'S 'ENGLAND' SPEECH (II.1.31–68)

Methinks I am a prophet new-inspired,
And thus, expiring, do foretell of him:

...

Ah, would the scandal vanish with my life,
How happy then were my ensuing death!

At the end of Act I Richard had received the news that 'Old John of Gaunt is grievous sick' (I.4.54) and, immediately formulating the plan to seize Gaunt's estate should he die, Richard had reacted with callous indifference: 'Pray God we may make haste and come too late!' (I.4.64). Act II opens with Gaunt anticipating a visit from the King in order that 'I may breathe my last / In wholesome counsel to his unstaid youth' (II.1.1–2). In view of Richard's immediately preceding words, to the audience this seems a futile gesture. Gaunt has hopes that, as the words of a dying man, his admonitions and exhortations to the King to mend his ways may at last have some effect (lines 15–16). His brother York, however, is of the opinion that Gaunt will be but wasting his breath. It is with wordplay on 'breath', on breathing in ('inspire') and breathing out ('expire') that Gaunt's speech begins at line 31.

The idea that dying men enjoyed a moment of extraordinary insight was common. Shakespeare gives it added point here in the compression of these lines. Gaunt has a vision breathed into him by God, which he now, like a prophet, breathes out as he speaks and as he literally expires (dies). Gaunt is known as an experienced counsellor of great integrity and his dying words would command attention, but, by alerting the audience to the oracular nature of what is to follow, these opening lines establish that this is a speech of still greater authority, an all but divinely sanctioned comment upon the actions of the King.

The lines which follow contain the first of many prophecies in the play foretelling that Richard cannot go on as he is without incurring dire consequences. The **images** stress the brevity of things bright and violent (lightning, fire, storms). They aptly reflect both the splendour of Richard's reign and its underlying cruelty (of which we have had an example in Gloucester's murder and the intended seizure of the Lancastrian estate). Gaunt then introduces the idea of over-indulgence and extravagance. Like the 'insatiate cormorant' (line 38), Richard will destroy himself. The lines are both a succinct characterisation of Richard's rule and a prediction of its inevitable self-destruction.

Then, at line 40, the speech assumes the quality of a vision. Gaunt moves from the failings of Richard to the prospect of the England which Richard so neglects and misrules. It is Gaunt's patriotic dedication to England which is the source of his anxiety about Richard's behaviour and which spurs him on to make one last effort to reform the King with his dying words. In Gaunt's mind, England is a place especially favoured both by nature and by God. That Gaunt believes this island enjoys special grace is conveyed by the **images** of paradise ('Eden') and jewels ('precious stone'), culminating in the phrase 'blessèd plot'. Running through these images are others suggesting England's natural advantages: the 'fortress built by nature', the 'wall' and the 'moat defensive' (the Elizabethan audience would remember how, only a few years before, the English Channel had prevented the success of the Spanish Armada in 1588). By the time of the climax of 'this England' (line 50), we have received an impression of it as a self-contained world ('little world') which enjoys all the blessings and lacks all the blemishes of the larger world beyond the sea.

Gaunt goes on to admire the people, and especially the royal and noble people, of this island. The 'happy breed of men' he had mentioned at line 45 are seen as literally the children of England ('this teeming womb'). By this Gaunt suggests that the peculiarly favourable conditions of England produce men with rare qualities. He concentrates upon the achievements of the English in the Crusades, and likens the extent of their reputation to that of the scene of the resurrection of Christ. This comparison both exalts the English and continues the religious thread in the speech.

The movement of this part of the speech reaches a climax in the repeated 'dear' (lines 57–8), an example of Shakespeare making fruitful use of the pun. The word captures both Gaunt's affection for this land (it is dear to him) and its value (it is of high estimation in the various ways Gaunt has mentioned). It is at this climactic moment that the speech abruptly changes direction. At the very moment that Gaunt is rapt with admiration for England he remembers the shame the country now endures under Richard, and the contrast is such that he breaks out in anger at the illegal practices of the King. And so the sea which earlier had been a defensive wall against the outside world now becomes a prison wall shutting in England's shame. England, unassailable from without, has conquered itself from within. The conquest Gaunt has in mind is, of course, moral, not military. This is consistent with the religious tenor of his earlier remarks.

By so effectively conveying the patriotic devotion of this old, experienced nobleman, the speech enhances the audience's estimation of Gaunt, which in turn renders his criticisms of Richard the more compelling. Consequently, the audience sides with Gaunt in the quarrel which follows when Richard enters at line 69. Furthermore, Gaunt's evocation of an England specially elected by God from among the nations would have appealed to the Protestant sentiment of an Elizabethan audience, whose members would be likely to regard Reformation England as ranged against the superstitious and tyrannical practices of such Roman Catholic countries as Spain. Gaunt's expression of patriotic sentiment would also have struck a chord with an England now discovering and asserting itself as a nation state. The speech is thus a touchstone of one strand in English Renaissance culture. Within the play, these various aspects are intended to range the audience against Richard in condemnation of his neglect of the land entrusted to him. It is the more shocking that England should be betrayed not by its enemies but by its anointed king. The speech thus creates in our minds a vision of England which will linger throughout the play. It is a vision which, at the play's end, it seems Henry will no more be able to sustain than could Richard. In that sense, Gaunt's words are a kind of valedictory to a world now vanished for ever.

TEXT 2 RICHARD'S SELF-CONSTRUCTION AS KING
            (III.2.36–62)

Discomfortable cousin, knowest thou not
That when the searching eye of heaven is hid

...

A glorious angel. Then if angels fight,
Weak men must fall; for heaven still guards the right.

It is characteristic of *Richard II* that, in contrast to the usual emphasis of Elizabethan history plays, it pays more attention to people's reactions to events than to the political intrigues and military actions which bring about those events (see also Plot & Structure and Characterisation). Hence, many of the main scenes of the play are scenes of discussion, reflection and analysis of the thoughts and feelings which circumstances have provoked. Act III Scene 2 is a case in point. Richard has returned from Ireland following Henry's invasion of England. The scene is structured around Richard's reactions as he is brought increasingly discouraging news of his situation. Richard had left for his Irish campaign at II.1.218–23, and has not been on stage since. During his absence the play has traced Henry's steady progress across England. By the time of Richard's return, we know his position is desperate: his followers have deserted him and been executed by Henry; his Welsh army has disbanded; York has joined Henry; both the general populace and the nobles have sided with the Lancastrians. In Act III Scene 2, the turning point of the play, we see the effect which news of these events has upon Richard. By the end of this scene, he has abandoned all hope, and Henry's success is assured.

The scene begins in an **ironical** mood for, having returned from Ireland, Richard is in an optimistic frame of mind, idealistically (and impractically) confident that merely his presence as King will be sufficient to win support and shame the rebels into submission. The audience, however, have seen the balance of power shift decisively to Henry in Act II and know that matters are much more serious than Richard realises. During the scene he comes to learn what the audience already knows, ·the true state of affairs. This scene marks the beginning of Shakespeare's concentration of the play upon Richard and his feelings.

Richard see-saws between hope and despair. As he lands at Barkloughly, he is overjoyed to be back in his kingdom. He conjures the earth itself to help him against the rebels in a speech which assumes that the world of nature will side with the true king. It is an affecting speech, but as Richard's followers immediately point out, not much to the purpose. Richard has never been able to appreciate that even an anointed king has need to plan his actions and assess their consequences. He banished Henry, seized his inheritance and used blank charters (see I.4.48), blissfully unaware (despite the warnings of Gaunt and York) that these deeds did not go unnoticed. So now the Bishop of Carlisle (Richard's noblest follower), while he agrees that God can indeed keep Richard king, nevertheless warns that human beings must take steps to help themselves (III.2.27–32). Aumerle stresses the point, claiming that it is their own negligence which has enabled Henry to achieve so much (lines 33–5).

Richard's reply, beginning at line 36, illustrates both his nobility and his folly. He rejects this advice as unworthy of a king – he has no need of policy: like the sun itself, kingly light can shame evil. The association between the sun, the brightest object in the heavens, and royalty, was traditional, suggesting the pre-eminence and the splendour of majesty. It recurs throughout *Richard II* (see Style on Imagery), with affecting and **tragic** aptness in the next scene when Richard likens himself to Phaeton, the son of the sun god Apollo of Greek myth, who was destroyed by Zeus for driving his father's chariot uncontrollably across the sky (III.3.178). For Richard, the **symbol** expresses his exalted notion of kingship, suggesting not only superiority and power, but also rectitude. As the 'eye of heaven' the sun, in Richard's conception, spies out misdeeds, exposing evil. Identifying Henry as a 'thief' and 'traitor', Richard is confident that when he, the royal sun, shines once more in England, 'His treasons will sit blushing in his face' and Henry will be shamed into retreat (lines 47–53). The **hyperbole** of this **rhetoric** is illustrated by the substitution of the Antipodes for the Ireland from which Richard has actually journeyed. Richard is continuing the comparison of himself to the sun (thought to travel around the earth, and so to cross the Antipodes at night), to emphasise the benightedness of a realm without its king (Richard supposes that, from the point of view of his English subjects, he has effectively been on the other side of the world) and correspondingly to exalt the magnificence of his return, 'rising in our throne, the east' (line 50).

In its final lines, the speech continues the same elevated theme, but now less **metaphorically**. Direct reference is made to Elizabethan constitutional and monarchical ideas in the references to an 'anointed king', 'The deputy elected by the Lord' and the immunity of a true monarch from judgement by his people (lines 54–7). These ideas were current at the time of the play's composition, and would become dominant in the next century under the Stuarts. They would fuel absolutism throughout Europe, most notably in the rule of Louis XIV of France, 'the Sun King', and would be a contributing factor in the outbreak of Civil War in England in 1642. In that conflict, Charles I and the Cavaliers maintained a doctrine of divine right monarchy, whereas the Parliamentarians sought an equal role for Parliament within the constitution. This lay far ahead at the time of Richard II, but these lines demonstrate all too plainly Richard's confident disregard of his people, dismissing 'worldly men' as inferior in degree to a king.

These lines also reveal the futility of Richard's position. His fond supposition that angels fight for him, while Henry has to press men into his service, betrays both a fatal misconception about the extent of Henry's support and an equally fatal and arrogant misapprehension about his true power. Kingship in itself has little hold over subjects unless the man who is king deserves loyalty. This is the fact which Richard has never grasped. His speech concludes 'Then if angels fight, / Weak men must fall'. However, the lines are unintentionally **ironic**: weak men shall fall, but not those Richard has in mind. Nor are we as sure as Richard is about which side the angels are on.

TEXT 3   RICHARD RESIGNS THE CROWN (IV.1.162–220)

Alack, why am I sent for to a king
Before I have shook off the regal thoughts

…

'God save King Henry,' unkinged Richard says,
'And send him many years of sunshine days.'

The moment when Richard formally resigns his crown and abdicates as king has been carefully orchestrated by the Lancastrian party. Its premiss is the fiction that Richard gives up his throne willingly: 'of thine own good will', as York puts it, Richard's 'tired majesty' abdicates (lines 177–80). The facts of the case, as Richard and the audience very well know, are quite different. The decorum and ceremonial of the scene is hence fundamentally unstable: what it represents, a voluntary transfer of power, is contradicted by the audience's knowledge of the coercive actions which have brought Richard unwillingly to this point. The scene is authentic enough as a transfer of power (Henry is now de facto king), but a charade as far as its representation of that transfer is concerned.

Throughout this passage, Richard plays upon this **irony**. His first words note the irony of summoning before a king someone who was himself so recently a king, and the word 'king' will echo through the ensuing lines like a refrain, repeated in a variety of contexts and with a variety of applications. Richard proceeds bitterly to reflect upon the trustworthiness of those who now pledge loyalty to Henry; after all, they had formerly sworn allegiance to him, and that oath now counts for little. An action apparently fair and just – Richard's surrender of his kingship – is deeply compromised by the treachery and hypocrisy surrounding it.

Richard develops this theme in a fashion characteristic of his exalted view of kingship. He likens his situation to that of the betrayed Jesus (lines 170–1). With his assurance that the King is God's deputy on earth, Richard would not find the parallel between himself and the son of God absurd, though it might strike an audience not only as **hyperbolic** and **melodramatic**, but also as verging on the blasphemous in its self-promotion. After all, Richard is certainly not divine, and hardly guiltless, as was Jesus. This is not a point which troubles his **rhetoric**. Quite the contrary: although Richard appears to salute Henry ('God save the King, although I be not he', line 174), the implication of the following line ('And yet Amen if heaven do think him me') is clearly that neither heaven nor Richard considers Henry rightful king.

Richard now takes the initiative entirely from those supposedly controlling the scene as he 'stage-manages' the business of passing the crown to Henry. Each of them holding it, Richard develops the **image** of the buckets, an image of inevitability which absolves him of all responsibility for what is occurring (lines 180–8). To this fine evocation, Henry can only lamely reply: 'I thought you had been willing to resign' (line 189). The contrast between his pedestrian style and Richard's sophisticated eloquence is nowhere more evident than in this scene, where it is to Richard's advantage since it introduces **pathos** into the proceedings by presenting him as a helpless (and guiltless) victim.

Richard's choice of the role of the weeper ('That bucket down and full of tears am I') is an important element in his self-presentation. It associates him with those other grieving figures in the play, the Duchess of Gloucester and, especially, Queen Isabel. He develops a contrast between the public realm over which a king rules and the suffering of a private individual, such as he has now become. In his powerlessness, Richard's is now what would have been regarded as the role of a woman in the play, able to react to events, to be hurt by them, but unable to control or direct them (see also Critical History on Feminist Approaches). This is the thrust of the wordplay on 'care' (lines 194–8). It depends upon a contrast between the public responsibilities of Henry now he is King, and the sorrow of Richard, now that he has lost the throne – between 'cares of state' and 'grief'.

Richard identifies himself so completely with the role of King that, deprived of it, 'I must nothing be' (line 200). The ingenious wordplay here involves a pun on 'Ay' (a **homophone** of 'I'). The words reflect both Richard's indecision ('Yes, no') and what he takes to be the denial of his identity which renunciation of his kingship involves ('No I'), his loss of himself ('I know no I'). Then Richard embarks on a majestically structured formal declaration of abdication, the **anaphora** inscribing the ritualistic nature of the laying-down of his majesty. Yet even here there lurks the pervasive **irony**: 'God pardon all oaths that are broke to me; / God keep all vows unbroke are made to thee' (lines 213–14) again highlights the treachery that places Henry in a position to receive oaths of loyalty. The salutation 'Long mayst thou live in Richard's seat to sit' (line 217) leaves no doubt as to whose seat it rightfully is, just as the audience, with historical foreknowledge of the play's end, is in no doubt that Richard will shortly lie 'in an earthy pit' (line 218).

Richard's **rhetorical** command of this passage enacts his kind of kingship: histrionic and performative. It works nowhere better to his advantage than here when, finally relieved of his responsibilities (the neglect of which was his downfall), he is free imaginatively to create his version of events, even as the event in which he participates has been determined by others. Regardless of political realities, Richard creates himself a king of suffering – a king Henry is powerless to dethrone.

PART FIVE

Background

WILLIAM SHAKESPEARE'S LIFE

There are no personal records of Shakespeare's life. Official documents and occasional references to him by contemporary dramatists enable us to draw the main outline of his public life, but his private life remains hidden. Although not at all unusual for a writer of his time, this lack of first-hand evidence has tempted many to read his plays as personal records and to look in them for clues to Shakespeare's character and convictions. The results are unconvincing, partly because Renaissance art was not subjective or designed primarily to express its creator's personality, and partly because the drama of any period is very difficult to read biographically.

What we do know can be quickly summarised. Shakespeare was born into a well-to-do family in the market town of Stratford-upon-Avon in Warwickshire, where he was baptised, in Holy Trinity Church, on 26 April 1564. His father was a prosperous glover and leather merchant who became a person of some importance in the town: in 1565 he was elected an alderman of the town, and in 1568 he became high bailiff (or mayor) of Stratford. In 1557 he had married Mary Arden. Their third child (of eight) and eldest son, William, learned to read and write at the primary (or 'petty') school in Stratford and then, it seems probable, attended the local grammar school, where he would have studied Latin, history, logic and **rhetoric**. In November 1582 William, then aged eighteen, married Anne Hathaway, who was twenty-six. They had a daughter, Susanna, in May 1583, and twins, Hamnet and Judith, in 1585.

Shakespeare next appears in the historical record in 1592 when he was mentioned as a London actor and playwright in a pamphlet by the dramatist Robert Greene. These 'lost years', 1585–92, have been the subject of much speculation, but how they were occupied remains as much a mystery as exactly when Shakespeare left Stratford, and why. In his pamphlet, *Greene's Groatsworth of Wit*, Greene expresses to his fellow dramatists his outrage that the 'upstart crow' Shakespeare has the impudence to believe he 'is as well able to bombast out a blank verse as the best of you'. To have aroused this hostility from a rival, Shakespeare must, by 1592, have been long enough in London to have made a name for himself as a playwright. We may conjecture that he had left Stratford in 1586 or 1587.

During the next twenty years, Shakespeare continued to live in London, regularly visiting his wife and family in Stratford. He continued to act, but his chief fame was as a dramatist and poet. From 1594 he wrote exclusively for the Lord Chamberlain's Men, which rapidly became the leading dramatic company and from 1603 enjoyed the patronage of James I as the King's Men. His plays were extremely popular and he became a shareholder in his theatre company. He was able to buy lands around Stratford and a large house in the town, to which he retired about 1611. He died there on 23 April 1616 and was buried in Holy Trinity Church on 25 April.

SHAKESPEARE'S DRAMATIC CAREER

Between the late 1580s and 1613 Shakespeare wrote thirty-seven plays, and contributed to some by other dramatists. The exact date of the composition of individual plays is a matter of debate – for only a few plays is the date of their first performance known – but the broad outlines of Shakespeare's dramatic career have been established. He began in the late 1580s and early 1590s by rewriting earlier plays and working with plotlines inspired by the Classics. He concentrated on comedies (such as *The Comedy of Errors*, 1590–4, which derived from the Latin playwright Plautus) and plays dealing with English history (such as the three parts of *Henry VI*, 1589–92), though he also tried his hand at bloodthirsty revenge **tragedy** (*Titus Andronicus*, 1592–3, indebted to both Ovid and Seneca). During the 1590s Shakespeare developed his expertise in these kinds of play to write comic masterpieces such as *A Midsummer Night's Dream* (1594–5) and *As You Like It* (1599–1600) and history plays such as *Henry IV* (1596–8) and *Henry V* (1598–9).

A new note is detectable in Shakespeare's work from the turn of the century. Plays such as *Troilus and Cressida* (1601–2) and *Measure for Measure* (1603–4), poised between comedy and tragedy, evoke complex responses. Because of their generic uncertainty and ambivalent tone such works are sometimes referred to as 'problem plays', but it is tragedy which comes to dominate the extraordinary sequence of masterpieces: *Hamlet* (1600–1), *Othello* (1602–4), *King Lear* (1605–6), *Macbeth* (1605–6) and *Antony and Cleopatra* (1606).

In the last years of his dramatic career, Shakespeare wrote a group of plays of a quite different kind. These 'romances', as they are often called, are in many ways the most remarkable of all his plays. The group comprises *Pericles* (1608), *Cymbeline* (1609–11), *The Winter's Tale* (1610–11) and *The Tempest* (1610–11). These plays (particularly *Cymbeline*) reprise many of the situations and themes of the earlier dramas but in fantastical and exotic dramatic designs which, set in distant lands, covering large tracts of time and involving music, mime, dance and **tableaux**, have something of the qualities of masques and pageants. The situations which in the tragedies had led to disaster are here resolved: the great theme is restoration and reconciliation. Where in the tragedies Ophelia, Desdemona and Cordelia died, the daughters of these plays – Marina, Imogen, Perdita and Miranda – survive and are reunited with their parents and lovers.

THE TEXTS OF SHAKESPEARE'S PLAYS

Nineteen of Shakespeare's plays were printed during his lifetime in **quartos**. Shakespeare, however, did not supervise their publication. When playwrights sold their plays to dramatic companies they sold their rights with them: copyright belonged to whoever had possession of an actual copy of the text, and consequently authors had no control over what happened to their work. Anyone who could get hold of the text of a play might publish it if they wished. Hence, what found its way into print might be the author's copy, but it might be an actor's copy or prompt copy, perhaps cut or altered for performance; sometimes, actors (or even members of the audience) might publish what they could remember of the text. Printers, working without the benefit of the author's guidance, introduced their own errors, for example by misreading the manuscript, and by 'correcting' what seemed to them not to make sense.

In 1623 John Heminges and Henry Condell, two actors in Shakespeare's company, collected together texts of thirty-six of Shakespeare's plays (*Pericles* was omitted) and published them in a large **folio**. This, the First Folio, was followed by later editions in 1632, 1663 and 1685. Despite its appearance of authority, however, the texts in the First Folio still present many difficulties, for there are printing errors and confused passages in the plays, and its texts often differ significantly from those of the earlier quartos, when these exist.

Shakespeare's texts have, then, been through a number of intermediaries. We do not have his authority for any one of his plays, and hence we cannot know exactly what it was that he wrote. Bibliographers, textual critics and editors have spent a great deal of effort on endeavouring to get behind the errors, uncertainties and contradictions in the available texts to recover the plays as Shakespeare originally wrote them. Modern texts are what editors have constructed from the available evidence: they correspond to no sixteenth- or seventeenth-century editions, and to no early performance of a Shakespeare play. Furthermore, these composite texts differ from each other, for different editors read the early texts differently and come to different conclusions. A Shakespeare text is an unstable and a contrived thing.

Often, of course, its judgements embody, if not the personal prejudices of the editor, then the cultural preferences of the time in which he or she was working. This has led recent scholars to distrust the whole editorial enterprise and to repudiate the attempt to construct a 'perfect' text. Stanley Wells and Gary Taylor, the editors of the Oxford edition of *The Complete Works* (1988), point out that almost certainly the texts of Shakespeare's plays were altered in performance, and from one performance to another, so that there may never have been a single version. They note, too, that Shakespeare probably revised and rewrote some plays. They do not claim to print a definitive text of any play, but prefer what seems to them the 'more theatrical' version, and when there is a great difference between available versions they print two texts.

Shakespeare & the English Renaissance

Shakespeare arrived in London when the Elizabethan period was poised to become the 'golden age' of English literature. Although Elizabeth reigned from 1558 to 1603, the term 'Elizabethan' is used very loosely in a literary sense to refer to the period 1580–1625, when the great works of the age were produced. (Sometimes the later part of this period is distinguished as 'Jacobean', from the Latin form of the name of King James I of England and VI of Scotland, who reigned from 1603 to 1625.) The poet Edmund Spenser heralded this new age with his pastoral poem *The Shepheardes Calender* (1579), while in the essay *An Apologie for Poetrie* (written about 1580, although not published until 1595) his friend Sir Philip Sidney championed the imaginative power of the 'speaking picture of poesy', famously declaring that 'Nature never set forth the earth in so rich a tapestry as divers poets have done … Her world is brazen, the poets only deliver a golden.'

Spenser and Sidney were part of that rejuvenating movement in European culture which since the nineteenth century has been known by the term 'Renaissance'. Meaning literally 'rebirth', it denotes a revival and redirection of artistic and intellectual endeavour which began in Italy in the fourteenth century in the poetry of Petrarch. It spread gradually northwards across Europe, and is first detectable in England in the early sixteenth century in the writings of the scholar and statesman Sir Thomas More and in the poetry of Sir Thomas Wyatt and Henry Howard, Earl of Surrey. Its keynote was a curiosity in thought which challenged old assumptions and traditions.

The rediscovery of many Classical texts and the culture of Greece and Rome fostered a confidence in human reason and in human potential which, in every sphere, challenged old convictions. The discovery of America and its peoples in 1492 demonstrated that the world was a larger and stranger place than had been thought. The cosmological speculation of Copernicus (later confirmed by Galileo) that the sun, not the earth, was the centre of our planetary system challenged the centuries-old belief that the earth and human beings were at the centre of the cosmos. The pragmatic political philosophy of Machiavelli seemed to cut politics free from its traditional link with morality by permitting to political decision-makers any means which secured the desired end. Meanwhile the religious movements we know collectively as the Reformation broke with the Church of Rome and set the individual conscience, not ecclesiastical authority, at the centre of religious life. Nothing, it seemed, was beyond questioning, nothing impossible.

Shakespeare's drama is innovative and challenging in exactly the way of the Renaissance. It interrogates (examines and asks questions of) the beliefs, assumptions and politics upon which Elizabethan society was founded. And although the plays always conclude in a restoration of order and stability, many critics are inclined to argue that their imaginative energy goes into subverting, rather than reinforcing, traditional values. They would point out that the famous speech on hierarchical order in *Troilus and Cressida* (I.3.86–124) or Katerina's speech on wifely submission to patriarchal authority in *The Taming of the Shrew* (V.2.146–60) appear to be rendered **ironic** by the action of the plays in which they occur. Convention, audience expectation and censorship all required the status quo to be endorsed by the plots' conclusions, but the dramas find ways to allow alternative sentiments to be expressed. Frequently, figures of authority are undercut by some comic or **parodic** figure. Despairing, critical, dissident, disillusioned, unbalanced, rebellious and mocking voices are repeatedly to be heard in the plays, rejecting, resenting and defying the established order. They belong always to marginal, socially unacceptable figures, 'licensed', as it were, by their situations to say what would be unacceptable from socially privileged or responsible citizens. The question is: are such characters given these views to discredit them, or were they the only ones through whom a voice could be given to radical and dissident ideas?

Renaissance culture was intensely nationalistic. With the break-up of the internationalism of the Middle Ages, the evolving nation states which still mark the map of Europe began to acquire distinctive cultural identities for the first time. There was intense rivalry among them as they sought to achieve in their own vernacular languages a culture which could equal that of Greece and Rome. Spenser's great allegorical epic poem *The Faerie Queene*, which began to appear from 1590, celebrated Elizabeth and was intended to outdo the poetic achievements of France and Italy and to stand beside Virgil and Homer. Shakespeare is equally preoccupied with national identity. His history plays tell an epic story, examining how modern England came into being through the conflicts of the fifteenth-century Wars of the Roses which brought the Tudors to the throne. He is fascinated, too, by the related subject of politics and the exercise of power. With the collapse of medieval feudalism and the authority of local barons, the royal court came to assume a new status as the centre of power and patronage. Courts, and how to succeed in them, consequently fascinated the Renaissance; and they fascinated Shakespeare and his audience.

That is why we are usually at court in Shakespeare's plays, and in the company of courtiers. But the dramatic gaze is not merely admiring; through a variety of devices, a critical perspective is brought to bear. The court may be paralleled by a very different world, revealing uncomfortable similarities (for example, Henry's court and the Boar's Head tavern, ruled over by Falstaff in *Henry IV*). Its hypocrisy may be bitterly denounced (for example, in the diatribes of the mad Lear) and its self-seeking ambition represented disturbingly in the figure of a Machiavellian villain (such as Edmund in *Lear*) or a malcontent (such as Iago in *Othello*). Shakespeare is fond of displacing the court to another context, the better to examine its assumptions and pretensions and to offer alternatives to the courtly life (for example, in the pastoral setting of the forest of Arden in *As You Like It*). Courtiers are frequently figures of fun whose over-refined sophistication is contrasted with plain-speaking integrity. When thinking of these matters, we should remember that stage plays were subject to censorship, and therefore any criticism had to be muted or oblique: direct criticism of the monarch or contemporary English court would not be tolerated. This has something to do with why the plays are always set either in the past or abroad.

The nationalism of the English Renaissance was reinforced by Protestantism. Henry VIII had broken with Rome in the 1530s and in Shakespeare's time there was an independent Protestant state Church. Because the Pope in Rome had excommunicated Queen Elizabeth as a heretic and relieved the English of their allegiance to the crown, there was deep suspicion of Roman Catholics as potential traitors. This suspicion was reinforced in 1588 by the attempted invasion of the Spanish Armada, a religiously inspired crusade to overthrow Elizabeth and restore England to Roman Catholic allegiance. Roman Catholicism was hence easily identified with hostility to England. Its association with disloyalty and treachery was strengthened by the Gunpowder Plot of 1605, a Roman Catholic attempt to destroy the government of England.

Shakespeare's plays are remarkably free from direct religious sentiment, but their emphasis is generally Protestant. The central figures of the plays are frequently individuals beset by temptation, by the lure of evil – Angelo in *Measure for Measure*, Othello, Lear, Macbeth – and not only in the **tragedies** Falstaff is described as 'that old white-bearded Satan' (*Henry IV Part 1*, II.4.454). We follow their inner struggles.

Shakespeare's heroes have the preoccupation with self and the introspective tendencies encouraged by Protestantism: his tragic heroes are haunted by their consciences, seeking their true selves, agonising over what course of action to take as they follow what can often be understood as a kind of spiritual progress towards heaven or hell.

SHAKESPEARE'S THEATRE

The theatre for which the plays were written was one of the most remarkable innovations of the Renaissance. There had been no theatres or acting companies during the medieval period. Performed on carts and in open spaces at Christian festivals, plays had been almost exclusively religious. Such professional actors as there were wandered the country putting on a variety of entertainments in the yards of inns, on makeshift stages in market squares, or anywhere else suitable. They did not perform full-length plays, but mimes, juggling and comedy acts. Such actors were regarded by officialdom and polite society as little better than vagabonds and layabouts.

Just before Shakespeare went to London all this began to change. A number of young men who had been to the universities of Oxford and Cambridge began to write plays which made use of what they had learned about the Classical drama of ancient Greece and Rome. Plays such as John Lyly's *Alexander and Campaspe* (1584) and Christopher Marlowe's *Tamburlaine the Great* (about 1587) were unlike anything that had been written in English before. They were full-length plays on secular subjects, taking their plots from history and legend, adopting many of the devices of Classical drama, and offering a range of characterisation and situation hitherto unattempted in English drama. With the exception of Lyly's **prose** dramas, they were composed in the **blank verse** which the Earl of Surrey had introduced into English earlier in the sixteenth century. This was a freer and more expressive medium than the rhymed verse of medieval drama. It was the drama of these 'university wits' which Shakespeare challenged when he came to London.

The most significant change of all, however, was that these dramatists wrote for the professional theatre. In 1576 James Burbage built the first permanent theatre in England since Roman times, in

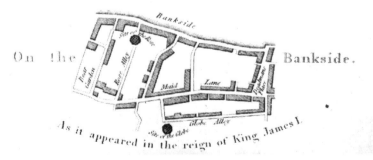

THE GLOBE THEATRE,

On the .... Bankside.

As it appeared in the reign of King James I.

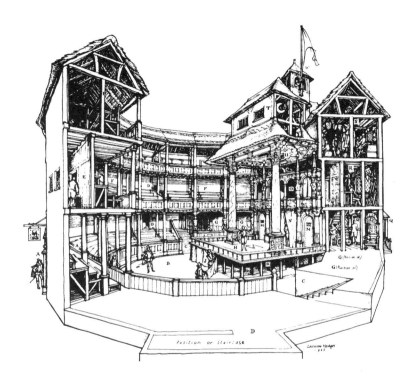

A CONJECTURAL RECONSTRUCTION OF THE INTERIOR OF THE GLOBE PLAYHOUSE

AA Main entrance
B The Yard
CC Entrances to lowest galleries
D Entrance to staircase and upper galleries
E Corridor serving the different sections of the middle gallery
F Middle gallery ('Twopenny Rooms')
G 'Gentlemen's Rooms' or 'Lords Rooms'
H The stage
J The hanging being put up round the stage
K The 'Hell' under the stage
L The stage trap, leading down to the Hell
MM Stage doors

N Curtained 'place behind the stage'
O Gallery above the stage, used as required sometimes by musicians, sometimes by spectators, and often as part of the play
P Back-stage area (the tiring-house)
Q Tiring-house door
R Dressing-rooms
S Wardrobe and storage
T The hut housing the machine for lowering enthroned gods, etc., to the stage
U The 'Heavens'
W Hoisting the playhouse flag

Shoreditch, just beyond the City of London's northern boundary. It was called simply 'The Theatre'. Others soon followed. Thus, when Shakespeare came to London, there were theatres, a flourishing drama and companies of actors waiting for him, such as there had never been before in England. His company performed at Burbage's Theatre until 1596, and used the Swan and Curtain until they moved into their own new theatre, the Globe, in 1599. The Globe burned down in 1613 when a cannon was fired during a performance of Shakespeare's *Henry VIII*.

With the completion in 1996 of Sam Wanamaker's project to construct a replica of the Globe on its original site, and with productions now running there, a version of Shakespeare's theatre can be experienced at first hand. The form of the Elizabethan theatre had derived from the inn yards and animal-baiting rings in which actors had been accustomed to perform in the past. They were circular wooden buildings with a paved courtyard in the middle open to the sky. A rectangular stage jutted out into the middle of this yard. Some of the audience stood in the yard (or 'pit') to watch the play. They were thus on three sides of the stage, close up to it and on a level with it. These 'groundlings' paid only a penny to get in, but for wealthier spectators there were seats in three covered tiers or galleries between the inner and outer walls of the building, extending round most of the auditorium and overlooking the pit and the stage. Such a theatre could hold about 3,000 spectators. The yards were about 80ft in diameter and the rectangular stage approximately 40ft by 30ft and 5ft 6in high. Shakespeare aptly called such a theatre a 'wooden O' in the Prologue to *Henry V* (line 13).

The stage itself was partially covered by a roof or canopy which projected from the wall at the rear of the stage and was supported by two posts at the front. This protected the stage and performers from inclement weather, and to it were secured winches and other machinery for stage effects. On either side at the back of the stage was a door. These led into the dressing room (or 'tiring house') and it was by means of these doors that actors entered and left the stage. It would have been on one of these doors, locked by Aumerle, that both the Duke and Duchess of York knocked in *Richard II* (V.3.37, 73). Between these doors was a small recess or alcove which was curtained off. Such a 'discovery place' served, for example, for Juliet's bedroom when in Act IV Scene 4 of *Romeo and Juliet* the Nurse went to the back of the stage and drew the curtain to find Juliet apparently dead on her bed. Above the discovery place was a balcony, used for the famous balcony scenes of *Romeo and Juliet* (II.2 and III.5). The balcony would have been utilised several times in Elizabethan productions of *Richard II*. In Act I Scene 1 Richard would have been seated there with his nobles, while Henry and Mowbray argued on the main stage below (at I.1.186 Richard asks Henry to 'throw up' to him his gage). In Act I Scene 3 Richard would again have been on the balcony, for at I.3.54 he 'descends' to embrace Henry, which he could have done by using the stairs which led down to the tiring house and then passing through one of the rear doors onto the stage. Most effectively of all, at III.3.61, when Henry and his followers see Richard come out on the battlements of Flint Castle, it would have been on the balcony that he appeared. And when, at line 178, Richard comes down to meet Henry with the words 'Down, down I come like glistering Phaeton', the fact that he did actually descend would have stressed the **symbolism** of the moment, with Richard coming down from his high place as king. Actors had access to the area beneath the stage; from here, in the 'cellarage', would have come the voice of the ghost of Hamlet's father (*Hamlet*, II.1.150–82).

On these stages there was very little in the way of scenery or props – there was nowhere to store them (there were no wings in this theatre) nor any way to set them up (no tabs across the stage), and in any case, productions had to be transportable for performance at court or at noble houses. The stage was bare, which is why characters often tell us where they are: there was nothing on the stage to indicate location. It is also why location is so rarely topographical, and much more often **symbolic**. It suggests a dramatic mood or situation, rather than a place.

None of the plays printed in Shakespeare's lifetime marks act or scene divisions. These have been introduced by later editors, but they should not mislead us into supposing that there was any break in Elizabethan performances such as might happen today, while the curtains are closed and the set is changed. The staging of Elizabethan plays was continuous, with the many short 'scenes' of which Shakespeare's plays are often constructed following one another in quick succession. That is why, in *Richard II*, Gaunt leaves at I.1.195, before the scene ends, in order to be ready to begin Scene 2, which would follow immediately. Production was much faster than we are generally used to today: in the prologues to

Romeo and Juliet (line 12) and *Henry VIII* (line 13) Shakespeare speaks of only two hours as the playing time.

Production was also more fluid than in the modern theatre. The location represented by the stage can change before the audience's eyes. During the first part of Act III Scene 3 of *Richard II*, Richard is on the castle battlements (that is, on the balcony overlooking the stage) while Henry and his followers are outside the castle walls (that is, on the main stage). However, when Richard comes down to meet Henry in a courtyard of the castle (lines 178–82), he enters the main stage and meets Henry there, so that now the main stage represents the interior of the castle. The stage has thus served as two locations (outside and inside the castle walls), but the acting has continued regardless. Henry and his followers have not moved; the scene has moved around them.

It is because of this continuous staging and the lack of scenery that characters in Shakespeare's plays often tell the audience what locality the stage represents at different moments. At the end of Act I Scene 1, Richard announces that the trial by combat which is to take place in Act I Scene 3 is to be held at Coventry (I.1.198–9), and Gaunt reminds us of this at I.2.56. At I.4.58, Bushy informs Richard that the dying Gaunt is at Ely House, so the audience is able to locate the next scene, in which Gaunt is carried onto the stage. At the end of Act II Scene 3 we learn that Henry will go to Bristol Castle, which is where Act III Scene 1 is set (II.3.163); and at the end of Act III Scene 2 Richard resolves to retreat to Flint Castle, where Act III Scene 3 takes place (III.2.209). Modern editors often supply a locale for scenes when the text fails to specify it, placing the first scene of *Richard II*, for example, in Windsor Castle, where the event depicted occurred historically, though Shakespeare does not mention this fact. It can be safely assumed that if Shakespeare's characters do not say where they are, then their location does not matter much.

The lack of a curtain across the stage in the Elizabethan theatre explains why scenes often end with rhyming lines (see also Style on Rhyme). These show the audience that the scene has ended, and prepare them for a new scene. And because actors were in full view from the moment they set foot on the stage, entrances and exits had to be written in as part of the play. Characters speak as they enter or leave the stage because otherwise there would have been a silence while, in full view, they took up their positions. Often, characters say that they are coming or going, to cover these movements (in *Richard II*, for example, I.2.74, I.4.63–5, II.1.221–3). Alternatively, a scene may begin in mid-conversation, with the characters talking as they enter the stage (in *Richard II*, for example, I.4.1, II.1.1, III.3.1). For the same reason, dead bodies always had to be removed by the actors in the course of the play: they cannot get up and walk off (Gaunt leaves the stage to die at II.1.138 in *Richard II*, and Richard's body is carried off at V.5.117 and V.6.51–2).

In 1608 Shakespeare's company, the King's Men, acquired the Blackfriars Theatre, a smaller, rectangular indoor theatre, with seats for all the members of the audience, facilities for elaborate stage effects and, because it was enclosed, artificial lighting. It has been suggested that the plays written for this 'private' theatre differed from those written for the Globe, since, as it cost more to go to a private theatre, the audience came from a higher social stratum and demanded the more elaborate and courtly entertainment which Shakespeare's romances provide. However, the King's Men continued to play in the Globe in the summer, using Blackfriars in the winter, and it is not certain that Shakespeare's last plays were written specifically for the Blackfriars Theatre, or first performed there.

R EADING SHAKESPEARE

Shakespeare's plays were written for this stage, but there is also a sense in which they were written *by* this stage. The material and physical circumstances of their production in such theatres had a profound effect upon the nature of Elizabethan plays. Modern fiction and modern drama are, by and large, realistic; they seek to persuade us that what we are reading or watching is really happening. This is quite foreign to Shakespeare. If we try to read him like this, we shall find ourselves irritated by the improbabilities of his plot, confused by his chronology, puzzled by locations, frustrated by unanswered questions and dissatisfied by the motivation of the action. The absurd ease with which disguised persons pass through Shakespeare's plays is a case in point: why does no one recognise people they know so well? There is a great deal of psychological accuracy in Shakespeare's plays, but we are far from any attempt at realism.

The reason is that in Shakespeare's theatre it was impossible to pretend that the audience was not watching a contrived performance. In a modern theatre, the audience is (usually) encouraged to forget itself as it becomes absorbed by the action on stage. The worlds of the spectators and of the actors are typically sharply distinguished by the lighting: in the dark auditorium the audience is passive, silent, anonymous, receptive and attentive; on the lighted stage the actors are active, vocal, demonstrative and dramatic. There is (again, usually) no communication between the two worlds: for the audience to speak would be interruptive; for the actors to address the audience would be to break the illusion of the play. In the Elizabethan theatre, this distinction did not exist, for two reasons: first, performances took place in the open air and in daylight which illuminated everyone equally; second, the spectators were all around the stage (and wealthier spectators actually on it), and were dressed no differently to the actors, who wore contemporary dress. In such a theatre, spectators would be as aware of each other as of the actors; they could not lose their identity in a corporate group, nor could they ever forget that they were spectators at a performance.

This, then, was communal theatre, not only in the sense that it was going on in the middle of a crowd but in the sense that the crowd joined in. Elizabethan audiences had none of our deference: they did not keep quiet, or arrive on time, or remain for the whole performance. They joined in, interrupted, even got on the stage. The plays were preceded and followed by jigs and clowning. It was all much more like our experience of a pantomime, and at a pantomime we are fully aware, and are meant to be aware, that we are watching games being played with reality. The conventions of pantomime revel in their own artificiality: the fishnet tights are to signal that the handsome prince is a woman, the Dame's monstrous false breasts signal that 'she' is a man.

Something very similar is the case with Elizabethan theatre: it utilised its very theatricality. Instead of trying to persuade spectators that they are not in a theatre watching a performance, Elizabethan plays acknowledge the presence of the audience. It is addressed not only by prologues, epilogues and **choruses**, but also in **soliloquies**. There is no realistic reason why characters should suddenly explain themselves to empty rooms – but it is not an empty room, of course. The actor is surrounded by people. Soliloquies are not addressed to the world of the play; they are for the audience's benefit. And the audience's complicity is assumed: when a character like Prospero declares himself to be invisible, it is accepted that he is. Disguises are taken to be impenetrable, however improbable, and we are to accept impossibly contrived situations.

These, then, are plays which are aware of themselves as dramas; in critical terminology, they are **self-reflexive**, commenting upon themselves as dramatic pieces and prompting the audience to think about the theatrical experience. They do this not only through their direct address to the audience but through their fondness for the play-within-a-play (which reminds the audience that the encompassing play is also a play) and their constant use of **images** from, and **allusions** to, the theatre. They are fascinated by role playing, by acting, appearance and reality. This offers one way to think about those disguises: they are thematic rather than realistic. Kent's disguise in *King Lear* reveals his true, loyal self, while Edmund, who is not disguised, hides his true self. In *As You Like It*, Rosalind is more truly herself disguised as a man than when dressed as a woman.

The effect of all this is to confuse the distinction we would make between 'real life' and 'acting'. The case of Rosalind, for example, raises searching questions about gender roles, about how far it is 'natural' to be 'womanly' or 'manly': how does the stage, on which a man can play a woman playing a man (and have a man fall in love with him/her), differ from life, in which we assume the roles we think 'appropriate' to masculine and feminine behaviour? The same is true of political roles: when a Richard II or Lear is so aware of the regal part he is performing, of the trappings and rituals of kingship, their plays raise the uncomfortable possibility that the answer to the question 'what constitutes a successful king?' is simply: 'a good actor'. Indeed, human life generally is repeatedly rendered through the **imagery** of the stage, from Macbeth's 'Life's but a walking shadow, a poor player / That struts and frets his hour upon the stage / And then is heard no more' (V.5.23–5) to Prospero's paralleling of human life to a performance which, like the globe (both world and theatre) will end (IV.I.146–58). 'All the world's a stage ...' (*As You Like It*, II.7.139).

PART SIX

CRITICAL HISTORY & BROADER PERSPECTIVES

TRADITIONAL CRITICISM

In Shakespeare's time, popular vernacular writing was not regarded as possessing the dignity of literature. The idea that plays in English which had been performed before a London audience might merit serious critical discussion was quite foreign to a period which still generally regarded Latin as the medium of weighty literary and scholarly endeavour, and which, in vernacular languages, reserved its applause for poetry modelled on Classical genres, such as the ode, the satire and the epic. The plays by Shakespeare's contemporary Ben Jonson, which were far more sensitive to Classical models and precepts than Shakespeare's, were in the process of changing this perception, but critical discussion of English Renaissance drama as literature does not begin until the late seventeenth and early eighteenth centuries.

Eighteenth-century criticism of Shakespeare was concerned chiefly with the structure of his plays and the extent to which this did, or did not, conform to the model of Classical drama, though the early eighteenth-century poet Alexander Pope, who edited Shakespeare's works, pointedly remarked that 'To judge ... of Shakespeare by Aristotle's rules [see Tragedy] is like trying a man by the Laws of one Country, who acted under those of another'. It was in reaction to the judgemental, and often censorious, tenor of much eighteenth-century criticism that the poets and critics of the Romantic period came to champion Shakespeare's genius, imagination and passion as far more important than matters of plot and structure. These qualities were discerned in Shakespeare's poetry, and in the authenticity this gives to the feelings of his characters. For the Romantic critic and poet Samuel Taylor Coleridge they were especially in evidence in *Richard II*. He held this to be 'the first and most admirable of all Shakespeare's *purely* historical plays' for its 'steady patriotism' and 'love of liberty' (with reference to Gaunt's speech in Act II Scene 1). In lectures on the play he commended the variety of its language, the individuality of its characters and Richard's 'high feeling of the kingly dignity'.

This line in criticism culminated in A.C. Bradley's immensely influential *Shakespearean Tragedy* (1904), which treated Shakespeare's characters not as parts of a dramatic design but as living persons, each with a personal history and a fully-developed psychology which could be analysed. He understood Aristotle's **hamartia** as a 'tragic flaw' in the character of the hero and interpreted the action of the tragedies in terms of the personality and choices of their heroes. His essays construct wonderfully full character studies of Shakespeare's tragic heroes (though his book did not include a chapter on *Richard II*). Bradley's approach was challenged in an essay entitled 'How many children had Lady Macbeth?' by L.C. Knights (1933). Knights rejected the assumption that it is the primary concern of imaginative writing to create literary characters and that the centre of Shakespeare's tragedies was therefore to be located in the personalities of their heroes. Knights argued instead that the plays are dramatic poems, to be appreciated not as fictions about believable characters but as texts whose poetry is their definitive feature. Knights showed how inadequate was the textual evidence to support such readings as Bradley's and how speculative such approaches are forced to become. In other words, there is no answer to the question 'How many children had Lady Macbeth?' but it is the sort of question which a treatment of her as a real person would be inclined to ask. The evil of the play, Knights argued, is poetically, rather than psychologically, explicable.

Equally traditional has been the supposition of nineteenth- and earlier twentieth-century critics that Shakespeare's art was wedded to stability, that the plays celebrate the beauty of harmony in the social and political orders, and that they are therefore politically conservative, on the side of the status quo, supportive of the structures of power in the state. This view was most influentially formulated in E.M.W. Tillyard's *The Elizabethan World Picture* (1943). Its view – that Elizabethan culture centred on a commitment to a stable world order reflecting the divine order of the heavens – has, in the last thirty years or so, been almost wholly abandoned by critics, who detect in the plays far more tension, irresolution, ambiguity and inconsistency than Tillyard discerned.

DECONSTRUCTION

Critical studies of the last twenty or thirty years have shifted the focus away from both order and character. Contemporary studies are concerned much more, primarily, with the complexity of texts and the way that their apparent meanings are contradicted and problematised. This **deconstructive** approach seeks to bring out the tensions within texts and to challenge the claim that texts have a single meaning, that which their authors intended them to mean. It is exemplified in the essays collected in John Drakakis's aptly entitled *Alternative Shakespeares* (1985).

Such an approach would focus on the ambivalence of *Richard II*, the ways in which the text constantly unsettles its readers or audience by preventing them from taking sides. The case for or against either Richard or Henry can be argued back and forth; the play's text declines to resolve the issue. Deconstructive readings would note, too, the open-endedness of the drama, and the **irony** that all its conclusion concludes is Richard's life. His death is so far from settling the power struggle with which the play is concerned, or from securing Henry's throne, that its consequences threaten instability for the foreseeable future.

The last words of *Richard II* illustrate how elusive the play's text can be. What can Henry possibly mean when he speaks of Richard's 'untimely bier'? He has himself acknowledged at the start of that very speech that 'I did wish him dead' (V.6.39). Nowhere in the text is Exton's claim that Henry had himself expressed a desire to be rid of Richard (V.4.1–3), repeated again now to Henry's face (V.6.37), ever denied. The murder is, then, a fulfilment of Henry's wish: Richard's death is actually very timely indeed for Henry. Does Henry perhaps concede that it was 'untimely' for Richard? Such a sympathetic thought in him seems improbable. And yet, even as he admits that 'I did wish him dead', Henry claims in this speech to hate both the deed and its perpetrator. How can that be? How can a person both want and not want something? Does Henry's reference to the 'untimely bier' actually conceal the recognition that political power is neither won nor held other than by corrupt means? What is 'untimely' is perhaps not so much Richard's death as Henry's realisation that he has now supplanted Richard not only as king but as political killer. The play had, after all, begun with Henry implicitly accusing Richard of the murder of the Duke of Gloucester. Here it ends with Henry implicitly Richard's murderer – perhaps little has changed after all.

HISTORICISM

Critics have also come to be more interested in the ways texts are shaped not by their author's intentions but by the societies and cultures which produced them, and in the extent to which they either reinforce, or work against, the political and social power systems of their time. **New Historicists** tend to argue that the status quo is confirmed by textual representations of power, while **cultural materialists** (often of a **Marxist** persuasion) such as Jonathan Dollimore look out for passages of resistance to institutional authority. Both are interested in how far the subversive tendencies of texts are contained.

Such approaches would seek to establish how far the traditional order has been re-established at the end of *Richard II*, how far it has been subverted, and how far reformed. It would ask whether the play constitutes a veiled critique of Elizabeth's absolutism, advocating some kind of restricted or constitutional monarchy or, at least, a recognition in monarchs of a responsibility to their people; or whether it is in effect propaganda for divine right monarchy. In short, is the play traditional or radical in its political allegiance? The centrality of Richard, the encouragement of sympathy for him through the **tragic** treatment of his predicament, the several defences of his rights as king and the prophecies of destruction and disorder should he be deprived of them, all make for the former view. So, too, does the rather inglorious start to Henry's reign in the quarrel which opens Act V Scene 1, the equally undignified squabbling Yorks in Act V Scenes 2–3, the threat of the Abbot of Westminster's plot, Henry's worry about his 'unthrifty son' (V.3.1), and the play's ending with his guilt and regret. When the King's throne is under threat, his nobles disunited, his dynastic prospects bleak and his 'soul ... full of woe' (V.6.45), the new regime seems hardly to deserve to be celebrated. On the other hand, however, there is a radical thrust to the comparison – wholly to Richard's disadvantage – between Henry's efficient exercise of power and Richard's self-indulgent, irresponsible and criminal rule. Gaunt's speech in Act II Scene 1 may evoke a romanticised notion of England, but it does so to enforce the audience's sense of Richard's betrayal of his realm and his people. Popular support is with Henry. To that extent, at least, the play has a democratic thrust.

The ambivalence with which both **deconstructive** and historicist readings of the play wrestle is epitomised in York's account of Henry and Richard's entry into London (V.2.4–21). His regal and chivalric **image** of 'great Bolingbroke, / Mounted upon a hot and fiery steed' and his impressive testimony to Henry's 'stately pace' as he rode through the streets receiving exuberant popular acclaim leave no doubt that this was a triumphal entry. This celebratory vein is, however, followed immediately by York's moving account (lines 23–40) of the scorn and derision heaped by the populace upon the 'sacred head' of 'gentle Richard', so barbarous and unjust 'That had not God for some strong purpose steeled / The hearts of men, they must perforce have melted' with grief. To applaud Henry and yet sympathise with Richard is simultaneously to approve and to disapprove of both men.

FEMINIST APPROACHES

A third strand in contemporary criticism is that of feminism. As a social and political movement, feminism is concerned with the status and roles of women in society, and particularly with the various ways in which women have been – and often continue to be – disempowered. In its literary dimension, it engages with textual representations of the female in order to bring to light their often unconscious ideological assumptions, their subordination and marginalisation of the female voice and experience, and their articulation of a masculinist agenda. It is concerned particularly with the ascription to women of a gender role which reinforces the idea that they are inferior to, or inadequate copies of, men.

A feminist approach to *Richard II* would first of all note how small a part women have in the play (only three female characters), and then that this role, in the duchesses of Gloucester and York and in the Queen, is, despite their elevated social status, exclusively domestic and private. They appear as a widow, mother and wife; their preoccupations are familial. Their business is to protect husband and child, and to that business the play allocates only a handful of scenes. In those scenes, motivated by wifely and motherly feeling, they plead for their husbands and son, seeking to divert from them the consequences of political acts which lie beyond the female sphere of influence. Those acts constitute the main action of the play, conducted by men. To that political and public action these women are peripheral, onlookers powerless to affect its course, as demonstrated by the Duchess of Gloucester's attempt to spur Gaunt to revenge in Act I Scene 2 and the Queen's attempt to remain with Richard at V.1.83–4. The Duchess of York does have more success persuading Henry to pardon her son Aumerle in Act V Scene 3, but in scenes of such violent emotion and frantic action that they are far removed from political seriousness.

Feminist criticism would highlight the fact that this is *why* these scenes are driven by women. Unlike the calculating and martial schemes of men, female responses in the play are characterised by sentiment and emotion. The Duchess of Gloucester is consumed with indignation and overpowered by grief in Act I Scene 2; 'True-love tears' are the currency of Queen Isabel (V.1.10). In Act V Scene 2, the Duke of York has a man's proper sense of public duty. To him, his wife is 'fond', 'mad' and 'unruly' in her refusal to obey him or to recognise the primacy of state affairs (V.2.95, 111). For her part, the Duchess is concerned only to save her son. Her perspective is defined by the experience of maternity: 'Hadst thou groaned for him as I have done / Thou wouldst be more pitiful' (V.2.103–4). This contrast accords exactly with the recurrent insistence in Elizabethan sermons and conduct literature that woman's place is domestic and private. It illustrates also the common belief that women are conduits of irresistible feeling. The play's language, in fact, identifies emotionalism with the female. Rationality, on the other hand, is masculine. 'Effeminate' is a disparaging epithet, used of men who fail to live up to the masculine ideal. When Henry is lamenting the unruly and dissolute life of his son, it is as a 'wanton, and effeminate boy' that he describes him (V.3.10) – that is, womanish in his lack of discipline, in giving himself over to pleasure. This kind of prejudice persisted long after Shakespeare's time. It is evident, for example, two hundred years later when Samuel Taylor Coleridge ascribes Richard's downfall to 'an intellectual feminineness which feels a necessity of ever leaning on the breast of others' and to his 'unmanly despair'.

Yet, even as it subscribes to this ideological prejudice, the play also raises questions about it: after all, Richard is the most 'effeminate' figure in the play, passive, imaginative, emotional. He of course pays dearly for this, but he is also much the most interesting and affecting male figure in the play. To the extent that he is able to hold our attention and win our sympathy the play constitutes a critique of the brusque masculinity of the Lancastrians which wins the day.

These various contemporary approaches characteristically each think of themselves as radical and committed to a left-of-centre politics; they believe that traditional readings of Shakespeare have been contrived (or 'fabricated') to support conservative thinking, traditionalism and the politics of the right. They believe that Shakespeare has been appropriated to serve the status quo (Prince Charles's publicly-stated admiration for him might be cited as an example). As Kiernan Ryan puts it in his lucid summary of these approaches in the opening chapter of his *Shakespeare* (see Further Reading), 'The problem is that so far the battle for the Bard has invariably been won by forces intent on fabricating from his life and art a powerful apology for leaving the world the way it is.' The belligerent **imagery** of Ryan's comment (criticism becomes a 'battle') suggests self-interest in traditional criticism, if not a deliberate plot; it is equated with 'forces intent' on resisting political change. One might remark that criticism such as Ryan's is still less impartial, his political commitment still more overt; but to this the reply would be that all criticism is political.

FURTHER READING

OTHER EDITIONS OF *RICHARD II*

The text referred to in this Note is Stanley Wells's New Penguin Shakespeare edition of *Richard II* (Penguin Books, 1969; reprinted with a revised further reading section 1997). The following editions of the play are also available.

Jessica Hodge, ed., *King Richard II*, The Arden Shakespeare, Nelson, 1996

> The standard scholarly edition of the play (superseding the 1961 Arden edition by
> Peter Ure), with a long introduction discussing the text, date, sources and literary

qualities of the play, and very full notes on each page which explain vocabulary, **allusions** and points of detail

Kenneth Muir, ed., *The Tragedy of King Richard II*, The Signet Classic Shakespeare, New English Library, 1963

> This edition has a useful general introduction to Shakespeare, an introductory essay to the play and glosses on the same page as the text. There is no commentary on the text, but there are helpful excerpts from critical studies of the play, a discussion of the text and sources, and long passages from the relevant sections of Holinshed (see Shakespeare's Use of Sources)

J.D. Wilson, ed., *King Richard II*, New Cambridge Shakespeare, revised edition, Cambridge University Press, 1951

> This scholarly edition has a readable introduction, a full discussion of the text, a stage history of the play, a passage from Daniel's poem (see Shakespeare's Use of Sources) and a glossary, but its notes have been superseded by Hodge's edition

SOURCES OF *RICHARD II*

See Critical Approaches for discussion of Shakespeare's use of the sources mentioned in these books.

W.A. Armstrong, ed., *Elizabethan History Plays*, The World's Classics, Oxford University Press, 1965

> Prints the complete text of *Thomas of Woodstock*

G. Bullough, ed., *Narrative and Dramatic Sources of Shakespeare*, in seven volumes, Routledge, 1957–73, volume III

> Reprints passages from Hall, Holinshed, *A Mirror for Magistrates*, Froissart, the *Chronique de la Traison*, Daniel's poem, and *Woodstock*, with an admirable introductory essay on Shakespeare's use of his sources

Kenneth Muir, *The Sources of Shakespeare's Plays*, Methuen, 1977

> Contains a chapter discussing the use of sources in *Richard II*

A. and J. Nicoll, *Holinshed's Chronicle as used in Shakespeare's Plays*, Everyman's Library, Dent, 1927

> Reprints relevant passages from Holinshed

GENERAL WORKS

Lily Campbell, *Shakespeare's 'Histories': Mirrors of Elizabethan Policy*, The Huntington Library, 1947

Discusses the relevance to contemporary Elizabethan politics of the ideas in the plays; a valuable, but not an introductory, book

Jonathan Dollimore, *Radical Tragedy: Religion, Ideology and Power in the Drama of Shakespeare and his Contemporaries*, second edition, Harvester, 1989

A **cultural materialist** account of Elizabethan drama as critically subversive

John Drakakis, ed., *Alternative Shakespeares*, New Accents, Methuen, 1985

A seminal collection of contemporary approaches to Shakespeare

Juliet Dusinberre, *Shakespeare and the Nature of Women*, Macmillan, 1975

An excellent introduction to the subject

Terry Eagleton, *William Shakespeare*, Blackwell, 1986

A lively and accessible account of Shakespeare in the light of **deconstruction**, **feminism** and **Marxism**

Stephen Greenblatt, general ed., *The Norton Shakespeare*, Norton, 1997

Much the most informative and critically up-to-date complete edition of Shakespeare available. Its text is taken from the Oxford edition edited by Stanley Wells and Gary Taylor (1986), but to this text is added a wide-ranging general introduction by Stephen Greenblatt, the foremost **New Historicist** critic, introductions to each play, notes and glosses on the page, an essay on the Shakespearean stage by Andrew Gurr, and an appendix of documents relevant to Shakespeare's life

Andrew Gurr, *The Shakespearean Stage, 1574–1642*, third edition, Cambridge University Press, 1992

The standard work on the subject

Lisa Jardine, *Still Harping on Daughters: women and drama in the age of Shakespeare*, Harvester, 1983

A **feminist** account of notions about, and the depiction of, women in the Elizabethan age and in Shakespeare, with many observations relevant to *Richard II*

W. Muir and S. Schoenbaum, eds, *A New Companion to Shakespeare Studies*, Cambridge University Press, 1971

> A collection of essays by different scholars covering such topics as Shakespeare's life, the Elizabethan theatre, Shakespeare's English, and his social and historical background

C.T. Onions, *A Shakespeare Glossary*, second edition, Clarendon Press, 1958

> A dictionary of Shakespeare's English, which explains the meanings of all words either not now in use or used in a different sense

John Palmer, *Political and Comic Characters of Shakespeare*, Macmillan, 1965

> Contains a traditional account of Richard II, following him through the play

Kiernan Ryan, *Shakespeare*, second edition, Harvester, 1995

> Surveys contemporary approaches to Shakespeare

S. Schoenbaum, *William Shakespeare: a Compact Documentary Life*, Clarendon Press, 1977

> The most authoritative biography available

CRITICAL STUDIES OF *RICHARD II*

N. Brooke, ed., *Richard II: a Casebook*, Macmillan, 1973

> A collection of passages on the play which includes extracts from all the major studies of it

J.R. Brown and B. Harris, eds, *Early Shakespeare*, Stratford-upon-Avon Studies 3, Edward Arnold, 1961

> Includes a lucid study of **rhetoric** in *Richard II* by R.F. Hill

Graham Holderness, ed., *Shakespeare's History Plays: Richard II to Henry V*, New Casebook, Macmillan, 1992

> Includes an essay by James L. Calderwood on the elusiveness of language in *Richard II*, and especially the meanings of such key terms as 'king'

Graham Holderness, Nick Potter and John Turner, *Shakespeare: the play of history*, Macmillan, 1987

> Graham Holderness discusses *Richard II* in relation to Elizabethan notions of history and the genre of the Elizabethan chronicle history

A.R. Humphreys, *Richard II*, Arnold's Studies in English Literature 31, Edward Arnold, 1967

Helpful introductory critical guide to the play

Naomi Conn Liebler, *Shakespeare's Festive Tragedy: the ritual foundations of genre*, Routledge, 1995

Has an interesting section on the significance of ritual and tradition in *Richard II*

M. Mack, Jr., *Killing the King*, Yale Studies in English 180, Yale University Press, 1973

Includes a sympathetic study of Richard

M.M. Mahood, *Shakespeare's Wordplay*, Methuen, 1957

A chapter on *Richard II* comments on the language of the play

Christopher Pye, *The Regal Phantasm: Shakespeare and the Politics of Spectacle*, Routledge, 1990

A **New Historicist** and **psychoanalytical** reading of Shakespeare's histories, including *Richard II*, in the context of the power structures and notions of sovereignty in Elizabethan England

Phyllis Rackin, *Stage of History: Shakespeare's English Chronicles*, Routledge, 1990

Treats *Richard II* in the course of a discussion of history, temporality and the relationship of Elizabethan theatrical production to Elizabethan historiography

M. Reese, *The Cease of Majesty: A Study of Shakespeare's History Plays*, Edward Arnold, 1961

Argues that Shakespeare was actively engaged in examining ideas of majesty and duty in the history plays; has valuable comments on Richard's notion of the divine right of kings

E.M.W. Tillyard, *Shakespeare's History Plays*, Chatto and Windus, 1944

A traditional study of Elizabethan views of history and the literary background to the plays; its argument that they are committed to hierarchical order and to the status quo in society and politics has been rejected by **New Historicist** studies

Derek Traversi, *Shakespeare: from Richard II to Henry V*, Hollis and Carter, 1958

The chapter on *Richard II* follows the course of the play and is enlightening on the earlier scenes and the character of Henry

World events	Author's life	Literature/drama
		1513 Niccolò Machiavelli, *The Prince*
1534 Henry VIII breaks with Rome		
		1548 Edward Hall, *The Union of the Two Noble and Illustrious Families of Lancaster and York*
1553 Mary I becomes Queen		
1558 Mary dies; Elizabeth I succeeds		**1558** Birth of Thomas Kyd
		1559 George Ferrers, William Baldwin et al., *The Mirror for Magistrates*
	1564 Born in Stratford-upon-Avon	
		1572 Birth of Ben Jonson
1576 James Burbage erects the first permanent theatre in England		
1577 Francis Drake sets out on round-the-world voyage		
		1579 Edmund Spenser, *The Shepheardes Calender*
	1582 Marries Anne Hathaway	
	1583 Birth of daughter Susanna	
	1585 Birth of twins Hamnet and Judith	
		1586-7 Raphael Holinshed, *Chronicles of England, Scotland and Ireland*
1587 Mary, Queen of Scots executed after being implicated in plot to murder Elizabeth		**1587** First performance of Marlowe's *Tamburlaine the Great*
1588 England defeats the Spanish Armada		**c1588** Probable first performance of Marlowe's *Doctor Faustus*
	late **1580s-early 1590s** Moves to London	
	c1590-3 Writes *Henry VI* (Parts I, II and III) and *Richard III*	
1592-4 Theatres in London closed due to outbreak of the plague		
	1593 Writes *Titus Andronicus*	

World events	Author's life	Literature/drama
	1594 Begins writing exclusively for the Lord Chamberlain's Men	**1594** Thomas Kyd, *Cornelia;* death of Kyd
	c1595-9 Writes *Richard II, Henry IV* (Parts I and II) and *Henry V*	**1595** Samuel Daniel, *The Civil Wars between Lancaster and York*
	1596 Hamnet dies; William is granted coat of arms	
	1597 First publication of *Richard II*	
	1598 *Richard II* reprinted twice	
	1599 Buys share in the Globe Theatre	
	1600-2 Writes *Hamlet* and *Twelfth Night*	
1601 Essex beheaded after attempt to overthrow Elizabeth I	**1601** *Richard II* performed at the Globe on the eve of the Earl of Essex's rebellion	
1603 James VI of Scotland succeeds Elizabeth as James I of England	**1603 onwards** His acting company enjoys the patronage of James I as the King's Men	**1603** Ben Jonson, *Sejanus*
1604 War between England and Spain ends	**1604** *Othello* performed	
1605 Guy Fawkes arrested after discovery of the Gunpowder Plot	**1605** First version of *King Lear*	**1605** Ben Jonson, *The Masque of Blackness*
	1606 Writes *Macbeth*	
	1608 The King's Men acquire Blackfriars Theatre; fourth quarto edition of *Richard II* is published	
		1610 Ben Jonson, *The Alchemist*
	1613 The Globe Theatre burns down during a performance of *Henry VIII*	
		1614 John Webster, *The Duchess of Malfi*
	1615 Publication of the fifth quarto edition of *Richard II*	
	1616 Death of William Shakespeare	
	1623 First folio edition of Shakespeare's works is published	

allusion a passing reference in a work of literature to something external to the work (such as another work of literature or a cultural belief)

anagnorisis (Greek: 'recognition') a term used by Aristotle to refer to the moment when a character discovers the truth about his or her situation; see tragedy

anaphora (Greek: 'carrying back') the rhetorical device of repeating the same words in several successive clauses, often at the start of a line of verse

blank verse unrhymed iambic pentameter

catharsis (Greek: 'purgation') a term used by Aristotle to describe the effect whereby an audience is 'purged' of feeling or tension, leading to a state of calm in which the hero or heroine's tragic fate can be contemplated without feeling of despair; see Critical Approaches on Tragedy for further discussion

chorus (Greek: 'dance') in Classical tragedies, a group of characters who represent ordinary people in their attitudes to the action which they witness as bystanders, and on which they comment. In later dramatic work, often single characters were given a choric function

closure the sense of completeness and finality achieved by the endings of some literary works (or parts of literary works)

couplet a pair of consecutive lines of poetry which rhyme together

cultural materialism a term deriving from cultural theorist Raymond Williams, cultural materialism is concerned with issues of class, economics and 'commodification', whereby it is argued that literature, which is supposedly separate from the marketplace of capitalism, is in fact the product of that marketplace

deconstruction most of the ideas of the theory of deconstruction originate in the complex works of the French philosopher Jacques Derrida (b. 1930). He believes that all notions of an absolute meaning in language are wrong; it should be the aim of the philosopher and critic, Derrida argues, to 'deconstruct' the philosophy and literature of the past to expose this false assumption and reveal the indeterminateness of meaning. See Critical History & Broader Perspectives for how a deconstructive approach might be applied to *Richard II*

euphony (Greek: 'pleasing voice') language which sounds pleasantly smooth and musical

farce technically, a specific genre of drama intended primarily to provoke laughter, using exaggerated characters, absurd situations and knockabout action; other forms of drama and literature more generally can contain farcical elements

feminism a tenet of feminist thought is that male ways of perceiving and ordering are 'inscribed' into the prevailing ideology of society. This can be disclosed by studying language itself, and texts, in order to discover the characteristic assumptions which are inherent in them. In patriarchal societies language contains binary oppositions of qualities such as active/passive, adventurous/timid and reasonable/irrational, in which, it is argued, the feminine is always associated with the less 'desirable' words in the pairs listed

folio (Latin: 'leaf') a large paper and book size: a printer's sheet is folded once to give two leaves (four pages)

hamartia (Greek: 'error, sin') a term used by Aristotle to denote the error of judgement made by a tragic hero or heroine, leading to his or her downfall

homophone (Greek: 'same sound') a word pronounced identically with another word, but spelled differently and having a different meaning

hubris (Greek: 'pride, arrogance') the self-indulgent confidence that, in Classical tragedy, causes a hero or heroine to ignore the decrees, laws and warnings of the gods, and therefore defy them to bring about his or her downfall

hyperbole (Greek: 'throwing too far') emphasis by exaggeration; hyperbolic language is common in everyday speech and in all kinds of literature

iambic pentameter a line of verse containing five iambs. An iamb is the commonest metrical foot in English verse, consisting of an unstressed syllable followed by a stressed syllable

imagery in its narrowest sense an image is a picture in words – a description of some visible scene or object. More commonly, however, 'imagery' refers to the figurative language in a work of literature, such as metaphors and similes

irony a use of language, widespread in all kinds of literature and everyday speech, which is characterised by saying or writing one thing while implying another. 'Tragic' or 'dramatic' irony describes the situation when the audience of a play is provided with more information about what is happening than one of the characters has – see the discussion of Tragedy in Critical Approaches

Marxism Marxist critical theory, based on the economic, philosophical and political thinking of Karl Marx (1818–83), considers literature in relation to its capacity to reflect the struggle between the classes, and to reflect the economic conditions which are considered to lie at the heart of human intellectual and social evolution

melodrama (Greek: 'song drama') originally the word 'melodrama' referred to any play with music; in the nineteenth century it began to be used more specifically to refer to a genre of popular theatre which tended to be sensational, with unsophisticated plot and characterisation and often bloodthirsty action, in order to easily shock audiences. The word 'melodramatic' is used nowadays simply to describe any writing which is naïvely sensational or 'over the top', particularly from an emotional point of view

metaphor (Greek: 'carrying over') a departure from literal writing which goes further than a comparison (or simile) between two different things or ideas by fusing them together: one thing is described as being another thing, thus 'carrying over' all its associations

motif a literary device, such as a theme, image or symbol, which recurs frequently, either within a body of literature or within a single work

New Historicism the work of a loose affiliation of critics who discuss literary works in terms of their historical contexts; see Critical History & Broader Perspectives

parody (Greek: 'alongside, mock poem') an imitation of a specific work of literature or style, devised so as to ridicule its characteristic features

pathos (Greek: 'suffering') a strong feeling of pity or sorrow

peripeteia (Greek: 'sudden change') a sudden reversal in fortunes. In the case of tragedy, the term can refer to the fall of a hero or heroine; or, in the case of comedy, it can refer to an abrupt change for the good. In non-dramatic genres it may be used of any sudden turn of events or reversal in circumstances

prose any text that is not patterned by the regularity of some kind of metre. It is contrasted with verse, which contains some element of repetition (for example in the use of rhythm or rhyme), creating a pattern

protagonist (Greek: 'first combatant') originally the first actor (and thus principal character) in a play; the term has now come to be interchangeable with 'hero', meaning simply the leading character

psychoanalytical criticism the application of theories of psychoanalysis to literature. Early psychoanalytic criticism involved attempts to 'read' the motivations of literary characters as if they were real people; by extension, literary characters were sometimes regarded as a means of access to the author's (presumed) psychological condition. More recent criticism, following the ideas of the French thinker Jacques Lacan, is concerned with the relationship between identity, language and desire

quarto (Latin: *in quarto* 'in quarter') a paper and book size: a printer's sheet is folded twice to make four leaves (eight pages)

rhetoric originally the art of speaking (and writing) effectively so as to persuade an audience; the term is now often used to cover the whole range of literary and linguistic devices

satire literature which exhibits or examines vice and folly and makes them appear ridiculous or contemptible. Satire is directed against a person or a type, and is usually morally censorious, using laughter as a means of attack rather than merely for the evocation of mirth or pleasure

self-reflexivity a 'self-reflexive' text is one that refers to itself – for example, a text in which the writer discusses the processes of composition, or in which the content of the text addresses the nature of the creative genre to which it belongs

semantics (Greek: *sema* 'sign') the study of meaning (of words or sentences)

simile (Latin: 'something similar') a species of figurative writing involving a direct comparison of one thing to another. Similes typically make use of the words 'like' or 'as'

soliloquy (Latin: *soliloquium* 'speaking alone') a dramatic convention which allows a character in a play to speak directly to the audience, as if thinking aloud about motives, feelings and decisions

symbolism the use of symbols in a work of literature. A symbol is something which represents something else (often an idea or quality) by analogy or association – a writer may use conventional symbols, which form part of a literary or cultural tradition, as well as creating new ones

syntax (Greek: 'arrangement') the grammatical structure of sentences

tableau (French: 'little picture') a pictorial grouping of persons in a drama

tragedy (Greek: 'goat song') a tragedy traces the career and downfall of an individual and shows in this downfall – which is typically due to a flaw in the individual's character – both the capacities and the limitations of human life

Author of this note

Professor N.H. Keeble is currently Head of the Department of English Studies at the University of Stirling, where he has taught for twenty-five years. During this time he has regularly run courses on Shakespeare. He has published widely on English literature of the sixteenth and seventeenth centuries.